ESL Grammar Handbook

for intermediate to advanced students of English as a Second Language

ALLAN KENT DART

The American Language Institute
New York University

D0202321

PRENTICE HALL REGENTS, Englewood Cliffs, NJ 07632

Library of Congress Cataloging in Publication Data

DART, ALLAN KENT (date)
  ESL grammar handbook for intermediate to advanced
students of English as a second language.

  Includes index.
  1. English language—Text-books for foreigners.
2. English language—Grammar—1950–   I. Title.
PE1128.D344   428.2'4   81–13947
ISBN 0–13–283804–4   AACR2

Editorial production, supervision,
  and interior design by Frank Hubert
Manufacturing buyer: Harry P. Baisley
Cover design by 20/20 Services Inc.,
  Mark Berghash

 © 1982 by Prentice-Hall, Inc.
A Simon & Schuster Company   fs, N.J. 07632
Englewood Cliffs, New Jersey 07632

Printed in the United States of America
10   9

ISBN 0-13-283804-4

Prentice-Hall International (UK) Limited, *London*
Prentice-Hall of Australia Pty. Limited, *Sydney*
Prentice-Hall Canada Inc., *Toronto*
Prentice-Hall Hispanoamericana, S.A., *Mexico*
Prentice-Hall of India Private Limited, *New Delhi*
Prentice-Hall of Japan, Inc., *Tokyo*
Simon & Schuster Asia Pte. Ltd., *Singapore*
Editora Prentice-Hall do Brasil, Ltda., *Rio de Janeiro*

to Linda

Contents

Introduction

ESL Grammar Handbook is a comprehensive survey of the English language for intermediate to advanced students of English as a second language. The book is appropriate for young adults at institutes, colleges, and universities, and for adults in continuing education programs. Young adults (16 to 18 years) in senior high schools would also find the material interesting and meaningful.

As the text tends to favor no particular place or culture, *ESL Grammar Handbook* is appropriate for those who are not living in the United States, the United Kingdom, or other English-speaking countries.

Although the order of the explanations has been carefully graded and sequenced, for advanced students it is not essential that the order of presentation be followed exactly as planned. However, for intermediate students (for whom much of the material may be new), I recommend that the order of the explanations be adhered to since the book is semi-programmed, and the old material is constantly being reviewed within the context of the new.

For each explanation in this book, there is a quiz in the *ESL Grammar Quiz Book.* To make locating a quiz easier, the number of an explanation in the *Handbook* corresponds to the number of its quiz in the *Quiz Book.*

This book can be used alone as a handbook. For example, in a writing class students need a handy reference to brush up on various points of grammar while the focus of their class remains writing. The Index will prove to be an invaluable aid to students at this time.

ESL Grammar Handbook can also be used in conversation classes, where confusion can arise over a variety of grammatical points. A quick referral to the *Handbook* might help to smooth out the flow of conversation; also, the explanations and examples in the material should make the conversation more lively and interesting. Again, the Index will prove to be an invaluable aid.

Formal and Informal Style

The terms *formal* and *informal* are frequently used in this text. Formal usage is that style found in formal writing; for example, in a written report to be submitted to the Security Council at the United Nations in New York, or correspondence in the world of business, government, or education. An informal style of writing would most likely be used in a letter to one's parents, a quick note to a neighbor, or a short story depicting everyday life. Compare:

> *formal:* Why do you not sit down, Sir, and rest yourself?
> *informal:* Why don't you sit down and take it easy, Bill?
>
> *formal:* To whom do you wish to speak, Madam?
> *informal:* Who do you wish to speak to, Ma'am?

People ordinarily use informal usage when they are speaking. Since the emphasis in the explanations is on spoken English, most of the model sentences reflect an informal style of writing. It is hoped that they also reflect that style of speaking used by a majority of people living in the United States today.

Acknowledgments

There are many people I wish to thank for the constructive criticism, encouragement, and interest they showed during the development of the manuscripts for *ESL Grammar Handbook* and *ESL Grammar Quiz Book.* I owe particular thanks to Fred Malkemes, a colleague and close friend of mine, and Anna M. Halpin, my good friend and former neighbor.

I must thank the administrations of the American Language Institute, New York University, and the English Language Programs, King Faisal University, Dammam, Saudi Arabia, for giving me their support and allowing me to test the materials in my classes.

To the following at Prentice-Hall, I wish to express my appreciation: Marianne Russell, Pamela S. Kirshen, Gloria Pergament, Ilene McGrath, and Frank Hubert.

For her many suggestions and the strong motivating force that she provided, I wish to express my indebtedness to Linda Markstein, Professor, Borough of Manhattan Community College, City University of New York.

I feel an especially strong feeling of gratitude toward the students in my classes at New York University who participated in various stages of development of the manuscripts over a period of two years. I would like to thank them all: Alex Kuropatwa and Adrian Scappini (of Argentina), Victor Hugo Rojas (of Bolivia), Jarslav Nehybka (of Czechoslovakia), Gloria Mendieta (of Colombia), Jesus Perez (of Cuba), Carmen Mariano (of the Dominican Republic), Omkathaum Yehia (of Egypt), Miriam Herrera (of El Salvador), Kriton Giordamlis (of Greece), Yeuk Xam Cheng (of Hong Kong), Mehrdad Razavi (of Iran), Fabio Cordi (of Italy), Kosai Fujioka, Tohio Fujita, Noriko Imai, Sachiko Kanai, Sutsuki Swawshima, Atshushi Kono, Suzuki Kyoyasa, Masayoshi Kawasaki, Kaoyo Myata, Yasamasa Ogisu, Hideo Tanaka, and Mihoko Tanaka (of Japan), Mahmoud Elder, Mazen El-Mani, and Maher Mohammed (of Jordan), Hae Sook Chung, Eum Young Co, Byung Yun Jun, Hong Don Kim, Sook Hee Kim, Hyun Sik Ko, Jong Doo Lee, and Pyong S Yim (of Korea), Yan-Wen Chou, Li Ming Bian, Hong Jun Kao, Cynthia Shiah, Jian-S Wang, and David Yang (of the People's Republic of China), Sandro Testino (of Peru), Nan-Kuang Chang, Ai Hwa Wai, and Shen-Yuh Wu (of the Republic of China), Milagros Alvarez (of Spain), Jamal Thwayeb (of Syria), Suwanna Luckanakul and Suthasinee Sirikaya (of Thailand), Myriam Alarcón, Sally Bohorquez, and Franco Delnardo (of Venezuela), and Andrew Dang (of Vietnam).

Allan Kent Dart
New York City

1   spelling plural forms of countable nouns

1. A COUNTABLE NOUN describes some *thing* that we can count:

    seven chairs   twelve oranges   a thousand years

Most countable nouns can be made plural by simply adding -s to the singular form:

    dream, dreams   book, books   lion, lions

2. Add only -s to nouns that end in -e:

    nightmare, nightmares   crime, crimes   prize, prizes

3. Add -es to nouns that end in -s, -ch, -sh, or -x:

    bus, buses   pouch, pouches   bush, bushes   tax, taxes

    Exceptions: Add only -s to those few nouns whose final -ch ending sounds like (K):

    epoch, epochs   stomach, stomachs   monarch, monarchs

4. Add -es to nouns that end in -z. When a noun ends in a single -z, double the -z before adding -es:

    buzz, buzzes   fez, fezzes   quiz, quizzes

5. When a noun ends in -y preceded by a consonant (all letters except the vowels *a, e, i, o,* and *u*), change the -y to -i and add -es:

    baby, babies   berry, berries   lady, ladies

Do not make a change when a noun ending in -y is preceded by a vowel:

    attorney, attorneys   pulley, pulleys   galley, galleys

6. For one-syllable nouns ending in *-f* or *-fe,* drop the final letter or letters, and add *-ves:*

> thief, thieves   knife, knives   shelf, shelves   wolf, wolves
>
> ***exceptions:***
>
> gulf, gulfs   safe, safes   belief, beliefs
> roof, roofs   chief, chiefs

7. We usually add *-es* when a noun ending in *-o* is preceded by a consonant:

> mosquito, mosquitoes   hero, heroes   potato, potatoes

Add only *-s* when a vowel precedes the *-o:*

> radio, radios   stereo, stereos   kangaroo, kangaroos

Add only *-s* when a noun ending in *-o* is a musical term taken from the Italian:

> alto, altos   soprano, sopranos   solo, solos   piano, pianos

8. Some irregular spellings are:

> child, children   goose, geese   ox, oxen   mouse, mice
> foot, feet   man, men   woman, women   tooth, teeth

The following three nouns have the same form in the singular and plural:

> sheep, sheep   fish, fish   deer, deer

Series and *means* also have the same form in the singular and the plural:

> the series is (are)   the means is (are)

Even though *people* and *police* do not end in *-s,* they are plural:

> the people *are*   the police *are*

9. A few nouns from Latin and Greek retain their original plural form:

> analysis, analyses   memorandum, memoranda
> aquarium, aquaria   oasis, oases
> crisis, crises   parenthesis, parentheses
> axis, axes   phenomenon, phenomena
> criterion, criteria   radius, radii
> datum, data   stimulus, stimuli
> hypothesis, hypotheses   thesis, theses
> medium, media

> **Note:** *Data,* the plural form of *datum,* is often thought of as singular as well as plural:

This data *is* wrong.   These data *are* correct.

2 distinguishing countable from uncountable nouns

1. An UNCOUNTABLE NOUN describes some *thing* that we cannot count:

> Give me *liberty* or give me death. (Patrick Henry)
> They won their *independence* after years of *revolution*.

The nouns *liberty, independence,* and *revolution* as ideas or concepts cannot be counted. Such nouns are also called ABSTRACT NOUNS.

2. Many CONCRETE NOUNS (things which we can see, touch, or smell) are uncountable:

> In the desert *water* is more precious than *oil*.
> How much *gold* is there deposited at Fort Knox?

However, we can count: two *glasses* of water, three *barrels* of oil, and *four* ounces of gold.

3. Quite a few countable nouns may be made uncountable, but a change in meaning takes place (occurs). Compare:

uncountable	*countable*
We will protect our *liberty*.	Their child has too many *liberties*.
Death is a mystery.	There were many *deaths* in the battle.
Love is eternal.	The *loves* of Cleopatra were many and varied.

4. An uncountable noun does not have a plural form; however, a few end in *-s:*

> *Politics* is a fascinating subject.   Is *mathematics* your favorite subject?
> The *news* is good today.   *Physics* tells us a lot about the world.

5. A COLLECTIVE NOUN describes a group of people, animals, or objects that is considered a single unit. In American English when a collective noun is used as the subject of a sentence, it usually takes a singular form:

> My *family lives* in California.   The *group is* ready to go on.
> The *class studies* hard.   The *herd is* restless tonight.

Note: A PROPER NOUN always begins with a capital letter.

Some kinds of proper nouns are:

a. Personal names:

> Mahatma Gandhi   Helen Keller   Charlie Chaplin

b. Geographical names:

> India   America   the Equator   Earth

    c. Names of languages, nationalities, and religions:

    English   an American   Buddhism   Christianity
    Russian   a Russian   Islam   Hinduism

    d. Names of state, national, and religious holidays:

    Labor Day   Independence Day   Christmas   Ramadan

    e. The days and months of the year:

    Saturday   Sunday   May   October

Note that the seasons of the year are not proper nouns and always begin with a small letter:

    spring   summer   fall (autumn)   winter

3   the possessive form of nouns

1. The possessive form of nouns (the possessive case) is formed in a variety of ways.

    a. For singular nouns and indefinite pronouns, add an APOSTROPHE (') + an s:

    my sister's bike   everyone's class   John's smile

    b. With singular proper names ending in s, you may add an apostrophe only:

    Betsy Jones' book   Charles' mother   Mrs. Williams' house

However, 's is more common:

    Mr. Jones's son   Carlos's family   the Williams's teenager

    c. It is customary to add only an apostrophe to *Jesus* and *Moses:*

    Jesus' life (but *the life of Jesus*)   Moses' people (but *the law of Moses*)

    d. Add only the apostrophe for plural nouns ending in s:

    my friends' friends   the boys' bikes   the babies' toys

    e. Add both the apostrophe and s for plural nouns not ending in s:

    the children's playroom   the women's room   the men's dormitory

    f. To show joint possession, the last noun is made possessive:

    Robert and his *roommate's* apartment (they share it)
    Tom and *Grace's* house (they own it together)

    g. To show separate possession, each noun is made possessive:

    Robert's and his *roommate's* bedrooms (they have separate bedrooms)

Tom's and *Grace's* children (they both have children from earlier marriages)

2. A possessive noun may appear without a following noun when that noun is understood:

the dentist's (office)   the locksmith's (shop)   Macy's (store)

3. A possessive form is most often used with a *person* or a *living being* (humans, animals, insects):

The *prophet's* prediction will come true in the year 2000.
How beautiful the *butterfly's* wings are!
My *cat's* tail is long and fluffy.

4. With things, we are more likely to use the phrase, *the . . . of:*

the color of your *eyes*   the width of the room   the weight of gold

However, a possessive noun is used with:

a. Expressions of time:

yesterday's blizzard   today's class   last night's dinner

b. Words related to natural phenomena:

the sun's rays   the ocean's tides   the moon's reflected light

c. Words related to political bodies or groups of people living or working together:

the socialist's position   the class's teacher   the nation's people

4   personal pronouns, demonstrative pronouns, and demonstrative adjectives

personal pronouns

	subject	*object*	*possessive adjective*	*possessive pronoun*
singular	I	me	my	mine
	you	you	your	yours
	he	him	his	his
	she	her	her	hers
	it	it	its	—
plural	we	us	our	ours
	you	you	your	yours
	they	them	their	theirs

personal pronouns

1a. SUBJECT PRONOUNS occupy the subject position of a sentence:

We are friends.   *I* was here yesterday.   *It* is late.

b. OBJECT PRONOUNS are used as the object of a verb:

They *know us* well.   He *sees her* every day at school.

Or as the object of a preposition:

She is in love *with him.*   I listened *to them* carefully.

Note: Subject and object pronouns often appear in compound subjects and objects.

She and I are engaged. This is a secret between *you and me.*

c. POSSESSIVE ADJECTIVES are used to modify (describe) nouns:

How good *his pronunciation* is!   How beautiful *your hair* looks!

d. POSSESSIVE PRONOUNS do not appear before nouns; they follow:

That book on the desk is *mine.*   This letter is *yours.*

They also occur as subjects:

Mine is on the desk.   *Yours* is still in the mailbox.

demonstrative pronouns

2. DEMONSTRATIVE PRONOUNS (*this, that, these,* and *those*), like subject pronouns, may occur as the subject of a sentence:

This is a map of Asia.   *These* are lovely flowers.

a. *This* refers to a person or thing close to the speaker:

This (watch on my wrist) was made in Switzerland.
This (gentleman) is my great-grandfather; he'd like to meet you.

b. *That* refers to a person or thing at some distance from the speaker:

That (car across the street in the parking lot) belongs to me.
That (woman up in the balcony) is my roommate.

c. *These* and *those* are the plural forms of *this* and *that:*

These (apples in my basket) are from our own tree.
Those (oranges up in your tree) are ready to pick.

demonstrative adjectives

3. When *this, that, these,* and *those* precede nouns, they are called DEMONSTRATIVE ADJECTIVES:

> *This book* is mine.   *These papers* are his.
> *That child* is theirs.   *Those flowers* don't look fresh.

5   prepositions of place

1. A PREPOSITION connects one part of speech with another:

> The books *on* that shelf are mine, and so are those *in* the drawer.

2. A PREPOSITIONAL PHRASE, which tells *where,* is formed by combining a preposition with a noun or pronoun:

> He's sitting *in the third row.*   John is sitting *between Chris and me.*

3. A PLACE PREPOSITION shows where a person, place, or thing is.

a. *In* suggests an enclosure:

> The keys are *in* my pocket.   My car is *in* the garage.

b. *At* refers to an area, a place, or an event:

> They're *at* the playground.   They met each other *at* a party.

c. *On* suggests a surface of some *thing:*

> Your shoes are *on* the floor.   Look at all the flies *on* the ceiling.

d. *Between* is for a person, place, or thing that separates two other elements:

> The Prince is standing *between* the King and the Queen.
> The beach lies *between* our house and the ocean.

e. *Among* is used for a unit of three or more:

> She was sitting *among* her friends at the meeting.
> Only a few men work in his office; he's usually *among* women.

f. *Around* refers to the encirclement (or surroundings) of a person, place, or thing:

> There are lovely trees *around* their house.
> Her friends are always *around* her during the bad as well as the good times.

Note: *In, on,* and *at* are sometimes interchangeable:

They are *at* school. (a place)	They are *in* school. (an enclosure)
We are *at* the playground. (a place)	We are *in* the playground. (an enclosure)
He's *at* the beach. (a place)	He's *on* the beach. (the *surface* or the *sand*)

4. An EXPRESSION OF PLACE usually contains a preposition + *the* + noun + *of*:

Their house is *in the middle of* a large forest.
Please put your name and the date *at the top of* the page.
There are a lot of notes *at the bottom of* the page.
The Appendix is *in the back part of* the book.
The Index is *at the back of* the book.
Is there a return address *on the back of* the envelope?
There is a lot of noise *in the center of* the city.
There is a large fire station *at the end of* this street.
My favorite grocery store is *at (on) the corner of* Broadway and 74th Street.
Please put that box *in the corner of* the room.
Children, please sit *in the row of* chairs *at the back of* the room.
There's a large blackboard *in the front of* our classroom.
There's a large sign *on the side of* their barn; it's an advertisement.
The First Lady always stands *at the side of* the President at receptions.

5. *In the front of* and *in the back of* may appear without *the,* but there is a completely different meaning. Compare:

They have a vegetable garden *in front of* their house. (they have a vegetable garden *outside* the house in the front part)
Their living room is *in the front of* the house. (their living room is *inside* the front part of the house)

Note: If you say their vegetable garden is *in the front of* the house, it means the garden is *inside* the house.

Slow down; there's a police car *in back of* our car. (there's a police car *outside* our car in the back)
We always keep a spare tire *in the back of* our car. (we always keep a spare tire *inside* the back part of our car)

6. Object and possessive pronouns frequently follow *in back of* and *in front of*:

Someone famous is standing *in front of me.*
My boss's desk is right *in back of mine;* his eyes are always on me.

7. The preposition *to* occurs in expressions of place with the adjectives *close* and *next:*

> Relatively speaking, the moon is *close to* the earth.
> At the zoo, the lions' cages are *next to* the tigers'.

8. The preposition *from* occurs after the adjective *far:*

> Our children are all grown up and *far from* home.

6   indefinite articles; *a* versus *an* before nouns and adjectives

1. *A* is called the INDEFINITE ARTICLE and appears before a singular noun or adjective that begins with a consonant sound:

> *A man's* home is his castle. (old saying)
> *A good* idea has just occurred to me.
> *A stitch* in time saves nine. (old saying)
> *A hot* cup of soup tastes good on a cold day.

2. *An,* the alternate form of *a,* occurs before a singular noun or adjective that begins with a vowel sound:

> *An elegant* woman suddenly entered the room.
> *An ostrich* thinks no one can see him when he buries his head in the sand.

3. A word beginning with a consonant letter usually begins with a consonant sound; however, certain nouns and adjectives begin with a consonant letter but have a vowel sound:

> She meditates *an hour* a day.   My neighbor is *an honest* person.
> It's *an honor* to meet you, Sir.   He's *an heir* to an oil fortune.

4. Most nouns and adjectives beginning with the consonant *h* have a consonant sound:

> a husband   a humorous   a house   a half   a home

5. *Herb* may begin with either a vowel or consonant sound:

> Rosemary is *an* (*a*) *herb.*

However, when the word is an abbreviation of the man's name *Herbert,* it begins with a consonant sound.

6. *An hotel* and *an historical* sometimes occur in American English, but their use is considered by many to be old-fashioned: *a hotel* and *a historical* are more common. *An* with these two words is chiefly British.

7. A few nouns and adjectives beginning with the vowel *u* have a consonant sound (pronounced *you*):

    a university   a universal   a useful   a unique

    a united   a union   a usual   a Ukrainian

However, most words that begin with the vowel *u* have a vowel sound:

    an ugly   an umbrella   an utterly

    an unusual   an unnecessary   an undercurrent

8. *European* and *one* begin with the vowels *e* and *o*, respectively, but have a consonant sound:

    They live *a European* way of life.   I have only *a one*-hour class today.

Note: *A(an)* can have the meaning of *one:*

    There's *a (one)* hair in my soup.   There's *an (one)* ant in the sugar.

One is almost never used to modify a singular noun. It is almost always replaced by *a(an)*. Also, *a(an)* can have the meaning of *per:*

    The crazy fellow was driving through town at a hundred miles *an (per)* hour.

Note: The following letters of the alphabet have a vowel sound:

    an *a*   an *f*   an *i*   an *m*   an *o*   an *s*

    an e   an *h*   an *l*   an *n*   an *r*   an *x*

7   "X article"

A or *an* is never used before a plural countable noun or an uncountable noun. We refer to this absent article as "X article" (or "zero article"):

    X Children are fun to play with.
    The love of X money is the root of all evil. (old saying)

8   noun modifiers

Nouns may be used to modify other nouns in much the same way that adjectives modify nouns. Like adjectives, noun modifiers do not have a plural form, and they always precede the noun they modify.

    They have a *gold brick* in their safe deposit box.
    I'm looking for a *coffee cup*, but I can't find one.

9 the simple present tense

1. The SIMPLE PRESENT TENSE is used for:

a. A generally known fact:

The sky *is* blue.   Water *contains* carbon.

b. A state of being:

The patient *is* alive and well.   We *are* in love with each other.

c. A habitual activity or occurrence:

The earth *revolves* completely every twenty-four hours.
The sun *rises* over those mountains every day.

d. A scheduled event in future time:

The plane *takes* off at dawn tomorrow.
The curtain *rises* at eight o'clock this evening.

2. *Am, are,* and *is* occur as the three forms of the verb *be* in the simple present tense. CONTRACTIONS of subject pronouns and *am, are,* and *is* appear in informal usage. A contraction always contains an apostrophe ('), which represents the missing letter.

	singular	*plural*		*contractions*		
1st person	I am	we ⎫		I'm	we ⎫	
2nd person	you are	you ⎬ are	you're	you ⎬ 're	
3rd person	he ⎫	they ⎭		he ⎫	they ⎭	
	she ⎬ is			she ⎬ 's		
	it ⎭			it ⎭		

3. The contractions *that's* (that is) and *there's* (there is) are commonly used, but contractions do not occur with noun subjects and the verb *be*; however, in speaking we hear a contracted form:

books are sounds like *books-er*
John is sounds like *Johns*
people are sounds like *people-er*

4. Except for the verb *be*, the BASE FORM (simple form) of a verb occurs in all persons except the third person singular:

	singular		*plural*	
1st person	I ⎫		we ⎫	
2nd person	you ⎬ work	you ⎬ work	
3rd person	he ⎫		they ⎭	
	she ⎬ works			
	it ⎭			

5. A base form + an -s is called an -s *form*. -S forms occur only in the third person singular in the simple present tense.

    a. Most base forms can be changed into an -s form by simply adding an -s:

        want, wants   eat, eats   run, runs

    b. Add -es for base forms ending in -o, -s, -ch, -sh, or -x:

        do, does   miss, misses   wash, washes

        go, goes   watch, watches   tax, taxes

    c. Double the -z in *quiz* before adding -es:

        quiz, quizzes

    d. When a base form ends in -y preceded by a consonant, change the -y to -i and add -es:

        carry, carries   bury, buries   fly, flies   ferry, ferries

    e. Do not make a change when a -y is preceded by a vowel; add only -s:

        stay, stays   buy, buys   play, plays   lay, lays

    f. Only the verbs *have* and *be* have irregular spellings:

        have, has   be, is

10   negative verb phrases

1. To make a negative verb phrase with all verbs in the simple present tense (except *be* and *have*), use the *auxiliary* verb *do* and the adverb *not* followed by a base form. *Does*, the -s form, occurs in the third person singular. *Don't* and *doesn't*, the contractions of *do not* and *does not*, appear in informal usage.

> **Remember:** The verb in the third person singular is always a base form in a negative verb phrase in the simple present tense.

1st person	I	} do not (don't) work
2nd person	you	
3rd person	he	
	she	} does not (doesn't) work
	it	

We	} do not (don't) work
you	
they	

2. To make a negative verb phrase with *be*, use the simple present tense followed by *not*. *Aren't* and *isn't* are the contractions for *are not* and *is not*. There is no contraction for *am not*.

	singular	*plural*
1st person	I'm not (am not)	we ⎫
2nd person	you aren't (are not)	you ⎬ aren't (are not)
3rd person	he ⎫	they ⎭
	she ⎬ isn't (is not)	
	it ⎭	

3. The verb *have* in the simple present tense can be made negative either with or without the help of the auxiliary *do*:

> I *don't have* time to help you today.   She *doesn't have* a place to live.
> I *haven't* time to help you today.   She *hasn't* a place to live.

The forms without *do* are chiefly British, however.

11   yes-no questions; pronoun substitutes

1. A YES–NO QUESTION asks for a simple YES or NO ANSWER:

> Are you a student? *Yes, I am.*   Is she a teacher? *No, she isn't.*

2. If the verb of a yes–no question is *be,* the verb begins the sentence. The subject is inserted between the verb and the balance of the sentence, which usually contains adjectives, adverbs, or prepositional phrases.

verb	*subject*	*balance of sentence*
Is	it	late?
Are	your parents	happy with your progress at school?
Am	I	a good friend of yours?

3. With all other verbs, the auxiliary verb *do* (*does*) precedes the subject in a yes–no question in the simple present tense. The verb, which is always a base form, follows the subject.

auxiliary	*subject*	*verb*	*balance of sentence*
Do	you	live	in or around this city?
Do	people	have	a good life in your hometown?
Does	he	do	his homework every day?

> **Note:** The verb *have* may also occur in questions without the help of the auxiliary verb *do:*
>
> *Have* you a dictionary?   *Has* she the correct time?

These forms are chiefly British, however, and do not ordinarily occur in American English.

4. In formal (and more polite) usage, we respond to a yes–no question with a yes–no answer. In writing, a comma appears after the *yes* or *no,* and a pause occurs in speech. The subject of the answer and a form of the verb *do* (or *be*) follow.

Yes, { I (you) do.   No, { I (you) don't.
       he (she, it) does.   he (she, it) doesn't.
       we (you, they) do.   we (you, they) don't.

> **Note:** Chiefly British: *Yes, I have; No, I haven't; Yes, she has; No, she hasn't.*

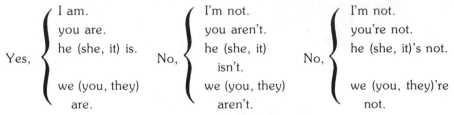

Yes, { I am.   No, { I'm not.   No, { I'm not.
       you are.   you aren't.   you're not.
       he (she, it) is.   he (she, it)   he (she, it)'s not.
                             isn't.
       we (you, they)   we (you, they)   we (you, they)'re
       are.   aren't.   not.

5. If the verb is *be,* contractions are never used with short *yes* answers, but they occur in long *yes* answers:

> Are you a student? Yes, *I am.* (*but* Yes, *I'm* a student.)

We most often use contractions in *no* answers:

> Are they students? No, they *aren't.* No, *they're* not.

However, for emphasis, we sometimes use the noncontracted form. Note that the stress is on the adverb *not.*

> Are you unhappy? No, I am *not.*   Is he a thief? No, he is *not.*

6. If the verb is not *be* (or *have* in British usage), a short yes-no answer never contains the verb expressed in the yes-no question; *do* or *does* is used to "echo" the verb. Compare:

	correct	*incorrect*
Do you like ice cream?	Yes, I *do.*	Yes, [I like].
Does she live here?	No, she *doesn't.*	No, she doesn't [live].

However, the verb occurs in long *yes–no* answers:

> Do you like ice cream? Yes, I *like* it. No, I don't *like* it.

7. The contractions *don't* and *doesn't* most often occur in *no* answers, but noncontracted forms are used for emphasis, as they are with *be* verbs. The stress is on *not.*

> Do they do all their homework? No, they do *not.*
> Does she have money in the bank? No, she does *not.*

8. To avoid repetition, we use PRONOUN SUBSTITUTES in statements or questions that are in response to other statements or questions:

Do *John and Mary like* it here?   Yes, *they* like it here very much.
Is *coffee* expensive now?   No, *it* isn't as expensive as it was.
John has *a new job.*   Does *he* like *it?*

9. A noun subject or demonstrative (possessive) pronoun in a yes–no question is almost always changed to a subject pronoun in the yes–no answer made in response to the question:

Is *Mr. Jackson* a hard worker?   Yes, *he* is.
Are *these* yours?   No, *they* aren't.
Does *Jack* have money in the bank?   Yes, *he* does.
Is *mine* correct?   No, *it* isn't.

12 information questions

1. An INFORMATION QUESTION (*wh* question) asks for more than just a simple *yes* or *no;* it asks for information. It begins with an INFORMATION WORD (interrogative pronoun) and ends with a question mark.

2. If the verb is *be,* the information word is followed by the verb, then the subject, then the rest of the sentence.

information word	verb	subject	balance of sentence
Where	are	they	now?
What	is	your name?	
How	are	you?	
Where	am	I?	
What	is	that blue book	on the desk?

3. If the verb is not *be* (or *have* in British usage), the auxiliary verb *do* (*does*) precedes the subject which is then followed by the verb and the balance of the sentence. As in yes–no questions, the verb is always a base form:

information word	auxiliary	subject	verb
Where	do	you	live?
What	does	that word	mean?
How	do	you	do?

4. The information word *what* is often combined with *color* + noun, or with *kind of* + noun:

What color car does your neighbor drive?
What kind of car does his wife drive?

Note: The preposition *of* never follows *what color.* Compare:

correct	*incorrect*
What color *eyes* do you have?	What color [of] eyes do you have?

13   expletive *there;* determiners

1. The word *there* is called an EXPLETIVE when it helps to introduce a verb (usually *be*) to the subject of a sentence. A DETERMINER (e.g., *a, an, no*) most often precedes the subject, which is then followed by a prepositional phrase.

expletive	*verb*	*determiner*	*subject*	*balance of sentence*
There	is	a	fly	in my soup.
There	are	no	people	on this ship except us.

2. The verb precedes the expletive in yes–no and information questions. The information phrase *how much* (+ uncountable noun) or *how many* (+ countable noun) often occurs in information questions.

information word + noun	*verb*	*expletive*	*balance of sentence*
	Is	there	a fly in your soup?
	Are	there	no people on this ship?
How much oil	is	there	in the world now?
How many gallons	are	there	in a barrel of oil?

3. The expletive in a yes–no question is repeated in the yes–no answer:

Is *there* a doctor in the house? Yes, *there* is. No, *there* isn't.

4. In informal usage, *there* is optional in information questions:

How many children are (*there*) in your daughter's English class?

adjectives and expressions that are determiners

5a. Some, any—*Some* and *any* may modify either countable or uncountable nouns. We use *some* in affirmative statements and in questions:

There is *some honor* among thieves. (old saying)
Is there *some milk* in the refrigerator?

Any appears in negative statements and in questions:

> There isn't *any cream* in the pitcher.
> Do you have *any fruit trees* in your garden?

b. Much, many—*Much* can modify only uncountable nouns. Rarely does *much* occur in affirmative statements in informal usage (perhaps occasionally in very formal written English). It is commonly used, however, in negative statements and in questions:

> Fortunately, there isn't *much trouble* in our town; it's quite peaceful.
> Is there *much agriculture* in your part of the country?

Many may modify only plural countable nouns. It occurs in affirmative statements, negative statements, and questions.

> There are *many deer* in these mountains.
> There aren't *many customers* in the store today.
> Are there *many sheep* on your mother and father's farm?

c. A lot of, lots of—*A lot of* and *lots of,* two expressions which have the same meaning, are informal substitutes for *much* (*many*). The expressions may appear before countable or uncountable nouns in affirmative and negative statements and in questions:

> There are *a lot of* (*lots of*) Cubans in the state of Florida.
> They don't have *a lot of* (*lots of*) money in the bank, but they're happy.
> Do you have *a lot of* (*lots of*) responsibilities in your company?

Note: As *much* rarely appears in affirmative statements, *a lot of* (*lots of*) occurs in the language more frequently than *much.*

d. A great deal of, quite a few—In rather formal usage, *a great deal of* can modify only uncountable nouns. The expression may appear in affirmative and negative statements and in questions:

> There is *a great deal of* oil in many parts of the Middle East.
> There isn't *a great deal of* sunshine in their apartment.
> Is there *a great deal of* corruption in the government?

Quite a few precedes only countable nouns. It occurs in affirmative statements and in questions, but not in negative statements:

> Do you have *quite a few* students in your class from Korea?
> We have *quite a few* fish in our aquarium.

e. A great amount of, a great many—*A great amount of* occurs before uncountable nouns, and *a great many* appears before countable nouns. Both expressions may appear in either affirmative or negative statements and in questions:

> There is *a great amount of* greed in the world.
> There aren't *a great many* older students in my class.

f. Little, few—*Little* may modify only uncountable nouns; *few* may modify only countable nouns. The two words do not occur in negative statements.

> There is *little* coal to be found in South America.
> There are *few* people in this town as nice as your parents are.

g. A little, a few—*A little* and *a few* occur more frequently than *little* and *few*. *A little* precedes only uncountable nouns; *a few* may precede only countable nouns:

> My company does *a little* research, but not much.
> Most everyone in my town is nice, but there are *a few* bad apples.

A little and *a few* show greater quantity than *little* and *few*. Compare:

> There is *little* money in my account. (almost none, perhaps a dollar)
> There is *a little* money in my account. (about a thousand dollars)
> There are *few* women in the class. (only two)
> There are *a few* women in the class. (seven or eight)

h. A little bit of—*A little bit of* is an expression that occurs in informal usage. It usually precedes an uncountable noun:

> With *a little bit of* luck, we'll get to church on time.
> There's only *a little bit* of salt in the soup.

i. No—The adverb *no* can be used as an adjective and modify both countable and uncountable nouns:

> There is *no* time to fool around in this office, Ladies and Gentlemen.
> There are *no* deer in the forest now; they've all died out.

We usually use *no* in questions to express surprise, anger, or irritation:

> ʾAre there *no* people in the world to help me during this crisis?
> Is there *no* peace and quiet in this noisy house? Quiet down, everyone.

> **Note:** *No* cannot modify a noun when a preceding verb is in its negative form. Compare:

> | *correct* | *incorrect* |
> |---|---|
> | She *doesn't have any* friends. | She [doesn't have no] friends. |
> | There *isn't any* air in here. | There [isn't no] air in here. |

Errors (mistakes) like *doesn't have no* and *isn't no* are called DOUBLE NEGATIVES; they do not occur in educated speech and writing.

14   infinitives; would like

1. The word *to* + a base form is called an INFINITIVE. Infinitives do not indicate person or tense. They often occur as objects of verbs:

> Our little boy *promises to be* good.   We all *hope to learn* a lot.

Here is a list of some verbs that are followed by infinitives:

agree	continue*	hope	love*	prefer*	start*
attempt*	decide	learn	need	promise	try*
begin*	expect	like*	plan*	remember*	want

> **Note:** The verbs marked with an asterisk (*) may also be followed by a GERUND. (= *ing* form of the verb):
>
> He *likes driving* (to drive) fast.   He *begins working* (to work) today.

> **Note:** When the verb *love* is used to mean *like,* it occurs in affirmative statements only:
>
> He *loves* to eat. (*never* He doesn't love to eat)

2. An infinitive combined with its complement, which is often a prepositional phrase, an adverb, or a noun object, is called an INFINITIVE PHRASE:

> My friends and I want *to build a sand castle down on the beach.*
> How would you like *to go on a trip around the world in eighty days?*

3. Infinitives may also follow nouns, or adjectives may follow combined with expletive *it* and a form of the verb *be:*

> Chinese isn't an easy *language to learn.*
> It isn't *easy to learn* a second language.

Frequently, *for* + a noun or pronoun is inserted between the adjective and the infinitive:

> It isn't easy *for the students* (*for them*) to remember the irregular verbs.
> It's good *for my roommate and me* (*for us*) to do exercises every day.

4. The auxiliary verb *would* combined with the verb *like* has the meaning of *want. Would like* may be followed by a (pro)noun object or an infinitive:

> I would like *a room reservation.*   I would like *to reserve a room.*

5. In informal usage, the contraction *'d* (*would*) can follow all subject pronouns except *it:*

> I (*you, she, he, we, they*) *'d* like to do a quiz now.

6. *Wouldn't,* the contraction of *would not,* occurs in informal usage in negative verb phrases:

> They *wouldn't* like to miss a class.   You *wouldn't* like to be in jail.

7. Yes–no and information questions with *would like* have the pattern shown in the chart below.

information word(s)	auxiliary	subject	verb	balance of sentence
	Would	you	like	to study French?
	Would	she	like	to marry me?
What	would	you	like	to do with your life?
What kind of job	would	you	like	to have?

Pronunciation note: *Would you* often sounds like *wood-jew.*

8. Short *yes–no* answers to *would like* questions are as follows:

Yes, { I (you) / he (she, it) / we (you, they) }   would.   No, { I (you) / he (she, it) / we (you, they) }   wouldn't.

Reminder: *Would like* does not mean *like;* it means *want.*

Note: The verbs *make* and *do* often occur as infinitives in the following idiomatic expressions:

Grandpa likes to *do a puzzle* every morning after breakfast.
Would you like *to make an appointment* with a hairdresser?

A detailed list of certain nouns that combine with *make* and *do* may be found in Appendix 2 of *ESL Grammar Quiz Book.*

15   impersonal it; duration with *take; last*

1. *It* is called IMPERSONAL IT when it is used in statements about:

a. Distance:

From the earth, *it* is sixteen million light years to the closest star.
Check the gauge; *it's* a hundred miles to the next gas station.

b. Identification:

Mr. Holmes feels *it* is the butler who stole Lady Smith's jewels.
It's Monday, and I don't feel like going to school.

c. Time:

What time is *it? It's* time to take a quiz.

d. Weather:

It's a cold, wet, and windy night. *It's* a warm, sunny, and balmy day.

2. When we wish to express the duration or length of an event, we use the following pattern: *it* + *take* (third person singular) + stated duration, + infinitive + balance of sentence.

> By train, *it takes four days to get* to Los Angeles from New York.
> If you have good weather conditions, *it takes two days to climb* to the top of that mountain.

3. An object can occur after *take,* but its use is optional:

> It takes (me) about twenty minutes to walk to school.
> It takes (*the students*) only a few minutes to do a quiz.

4. *How long* usually occurs in information questions with *take* expressing duration:

> On the average, *how long* does it take to learn how to speak and write English well?
> *How long* does it usually take you to do your homework?

5. *How many* + seconds, minutes, hours, etc. is also frequently used in information questions:

> Please don't be so slow, Dawn. *How many minutes* does it take you to make your bed?
> *How many hours* does it take to write a good composition?

6. The verb *last* means to continue in existence, to endure, go on:

> My grammar class usually *lasts* three hours.
> How long does a good automobile *last?*

16 adverbs

1. An ADVERB is a word used to modify:

a. A verb:

> He *sings beautifully.*   She *carefully selected* the best grapes.

b. An adjective:

> His voice is *very beautiful.*   Our neighbors are *quite poor.*

c. Another adverb:

> He always speaks *too quickly.*   My boss types *rather poorly.*

d. An entire sentence:

> *Fortunately,* our health is good.   *Obviously,* I am in love.

2. An ADVERB OF MANNER, which tells *how,* is made by adding *-ly* to an adjective:

 sly, sly*ly* childish, childish*ly* honest, honest*ly*

3. Adverbs of manner usually follow the verbs that they modify:

 He *explained carefully* the procedure.
 He *walked quickly* out of the room.

They sometimes precede the verb:

 He *carefully explained* the procedure.
 He *quickly walked* out of the room.

4. There are a number of rules for spelling adverbs derived from adjectives.

 a. For adjectives ending in a final *-y* preceded by a consonant, change the *-y* to *-i* and add *-ly:*

 easy, easily happy, happily crazy, crazily heavy, heavily

 b. For adjectives ending in *-ble, -ple, -tle,* and *-dle,* the *-le* is dropped before adding *-ly:*

 possible, possibly simple, simply gentle, gently idle, idly

 c. When an adjective ends in *-l,* keep the *-l* and add *-ly:*

 accidental, accidentally careful, carefully thoughtful, thoughtfully

5. The adverbs of manner *hard* and *fast* are exceptions: they do not end in *-ly.* They may occur as adjectives or adverbs:

 (*adj.*) He is a *fast runner.* (*adv.*) He *runs fast.*
 (*adj.*) We're *hard workers.* (*adv.*) We *work hard.*

Note: The adverb *hardly* means *scarcely* or *barely:*

 He *hardly* speaks English.
 I *hardly* know my classmates.

6. *Well,* the adverbial form of *good,* is another exception:

 She speaks, reads, and writes *well.*
 He runs, jumps, and swims *well.*

7. The *adverbs of time early, late, daily, weekly, monthly,* and *yearly* also occur as adjectives:

 (*adj.*) He's the *late worker* tonight. (*adv.*) He works *late* tonight.
 (*adj.*) She's an *early arrival.* (*adv.*) She *arrives early* every
                 day.

Note: The adverb _lately_ means _recently;_ it does not mean _not early._

8. _Right_ may occur as an adjective or an adverb:

He always has the _right_ (adj.) answer.
She does everything _right_ (adv.).

9. In informal usage, when we use the verb _drive_ in reference to automobiles, we may use the adjective _slow_ as an adverb:

Drive slow (_or_ slowly) through town, Sir; there are many busy intersections.

With all other verbs, use _slowly_ only:

Would you please repeat your question more _slowly._
It was a hot summer day, and the clouds were drifting _slowly_ over our heads.

10. The SENTENCE ADVERBS _fortunately, unfortunately, obviously, actually, really, presumably,_ and _possibly_ modify an entire sentence:

Presumably, the kidnapper's motive was ransom.
Really, are you in love with a woman in this class?

Note: In English, _actually_ means _really._ It does not mean _now_ as in some other Indo-European languages.

11. Sentence adverbs like _perhaps, possibly, probably, maybe, hopefully,_ and _absolutely_ act as one-word answers to a yes–no question:

Are you arriving at the meeting late? _Perhaps._
Does he expect money for his work? _Absolutely._

12. Adverbs of degree suggest an amount of completion:

The refrigerator is _almost_ (_completely, partially_) full.

_17_ linking verbs; adjectives versus adverbs

1. A LINKING VERB links (connects) a subject to the balance of a sentence. The linking verbs are:

be   appear   look   seem   feel   taste   smell   sound

2. Adjectives, not adverbs of manner, follow linking verbs:

They _are happy._
This sauce _smells good._
This ice cream _tastes delicious._

3. *Appear* and *look* are sometimes not linking verbs:

> This procedure appears *regular*. (*but* That actor appears on TV *regularly*.)
> She looks *graceful*. (*but* She looked *gracefully* at herself in the mirror.)

4. When *well* refers to a state of good health, it is an adjective and may follow a linking verb:

> (*adv.*) She dances *well*.
> (*adj.*) She looks *well*. (she is in a state of good health)

To feel *good* means *to be in a happy **mental** state:*

> I *feel good* about the terms in my new contract with the company.
> It's spring, the flowers are out, and everyone feels *good*.

To feel *well* means *to be in a healthy **physical** state.*

> Yes, Doctor, I *feel well*; I don't think there's anything wrong with me.
> Unfortunately, the teacher doesn't *feel well* today; she's gone home.

5. An adverb may follow *feel* when the verb means to have an opinion or a conviction:

> We *feel strongly* about equal rights for all minority groups in our society.
> He *feels differently* about politics now that he is older and more mature.

6. The adjective *bad* (not *badly*), meaning *sick,* is the proper form after the linking verbs *feel* and *look:*

> Unfortunately, the patient feels (looks) *bad* today.

In informal usage (sometimes in formal), *badly* may follow *feel* when the word means *regretful* or *sad:*

> We all feel *bad* (*badly*) about the poor people in our town.

Note: *Badly* always follows a nonlinking verb:

> She sometimes *speaks badly* of her roommate.
> He drank a little too much wine at the dinner party and *behaved badly*.

18 exclamations

1. An EXCLAMATORY PHRASE does not contain a subject or verb; it usually ends with an EXCLAMATION MARK (!). One pattern of exclamatory phrase is *what a* or *what an* followed by a singular noun:

> *What a* woman! *What a* man! *What a* clever fellow!
> *What an* honest person!

When the noun is plural or uncountable, the phrase begins with *what*.

> *What* women!   *What* fantastic photographs!   *What* sensational news!

2. *How* + an adjective (never a noun) frequently appears as an exclamatory phrase:

> *How fabulous!   How terrific!   How tragic!   How disastrous!*

3. An EXCLAMATORY SENTENCE is made by combining an exclamatory phrase with a subject followed by a verb:

> What a glamorous woman *your mother is!* What beautiful hair *she has!*

4. Only adjectives can appear in exclamatory **phrases** beginning with *how*; however, adverbs as well as adjectives may appear in exclamatory **sentences** beginning with *how*:

> How *strange* that man is! How *strangely* he's looking at people!

5. *Such* or *such a (an)* may replace *what a (an)* in an exclamatory sentence. When this takes place, *such a (an)* follows the subject and verb in the sentence:

> *They are such* beautiful children! *You're such an* honorable man!

Such or *such a (an)* also occurs in exclamatory phrases:

> *Such an* ugly picture!   *Such beautiful* flowers!   *Such a* problem!

19 frequency adverbs

1. FREQUENCY ADVERBS describe the frequency of an event and occur most often in the simple present tense. They are:

always	hardly ever	often	sometimes
ever	never	rarely	usually
frequently	occasionally	seldom	

2. If the verb of the sentence is *be*, the frequency adverb usually follows the verb:

> Our teacher *is never* late.
> Our neighbors *are rarely* home.

However, for emphasis, the adverb may precede the verb *be*:

> He *occasionally is* wrong, but not often.
> Grandfather *sometimes is* a little stubborn, but only once in a while.

3. With all other verbs, the frequency adverb always precedes the verb:

> The teacher *often gets* to class before me.
> The weather has been unpredictable; I *seldom have* my umbrella when it rains.

Sentences with frequency adverbs have the following pattern:

subject	adverb	verb	adverb	balance of sentence
The students	(always)	are	always	on time for class.
She	(sometimes)	is	sometimes	a little angry with him.
He	hardly ever	makes	X	a mistake when he writes.
We	rarely	go	X	hiking when it rains.

> **Pronunciation Note:** *Often* frequently sounds like *ah-fen;* the *t* is silent; however, *often* may be pronounced several ways in the United States.

4. In a negative verb phrase in the simple present tense, a frequency adverb precedes a base form unless the verb is *be:*

> My parents do not *often go* to church on Sundays.
> My roommate doesn't *ever waste* time at school; he's an excellent student.
> May in Paris *isn't always* nice; it sometimes rains a lot.

5. The frequency adverb *ever* occurs in negative verb phrases only. *Always, often,* and *usually* may occur in either affirmative or negative verb phrases. These adverbs usually follow the verb *be* + *not:*

> It *isn't ever* cold in Hawaii.
> It *isn't usually* windy in May.

For emphasis, they sometimes precede the verb *be:*

> She *often isn't* at the office on time in the mornings, but she gets here sooner or later.
> My boss *usually isn't* on time; he depends on me to do everything in the mornings.

6. *Isn't ever* means *never is:*

> A really good cigar *isn't ever* (*never is*) cheap.

Isn't always means *usually is:*

> The teacher *isn't always* (*usually is*) on time.

Isn't usually (isn't often) means *rarely is* or *seldom is:*

> Our house *isn't usually (rarely is)* busy on Sunday mornings; everyone in the family prefers to sleep late.

Doesn't ever do means *never does:*

> He *doesn't ever do (never does)* any homework, but he does well in class.

Doesn't always make means *usually makes:*

> My company *doesn't always make (usually makes)* very high profits.

Doesn't usually (doesn't often) have means *rarely (seldom) has:*

> My mother *doesn't usually have (rarely has)* coffee in the mornings.

7. The adverb *almost* is frequently used to qualify *always:*

> I usually vote for a Democrat, but my roommate *almost always* votes for a Republican.
> At the theater in New York, the curtain *almost always* rises on time.

8. The idiom *hardly ever* means *almost never:*

> She *hardly ever (almost never)* goes to bed before midnight.
> Phoenix, Arizona is very dry; it *hardly ever (almost never)* rains.

9. *Most* is often used to intensify *frequently* and *often:*

> The panda is *most frequently (most often)* found at high altitudes.

20 yes-no questions with frequency adverbs

1. In yes–no questions with the verb *be* in the simple present tense, frequency adverbs follow the subject:

verb	*subject*	*adverb*	*balance of sentence*
Is	the weather	always	nice at this time of the year?
Are	the students	usually	on time in the mornings?
Am	I	ever	wrong in my decisions?

2. In questions with the verb *be* and expletive *there,* frequency adverbs follow the expletive:

verb	*expletive*	*adverb*	*subject*	*balance of sentence*
Are	there	always	a lot of people	at the meetings?
Is	there	usually	much rain	during April?

3. As with the verb *be*, with other verbs, frequency adverbs follow the subject in questions in the simple present tense:

auxiliary	subject	adverb	verb	balance of sentence
Do	you	ever	forget	to brush your teeth?
Does	time	usually	go	fast in your class?

21   information questions with frequency adverbs

1. *How often* or *how frequently* is commonly used in information questions in the simple present tense to ask for the frequency of an event.

2. The pattern of information questions with the verb *be* and frequency adverbs is as follows:

information word(s)	verb	subject	adverb	balance of sentence
How often	is	your class?		
What time	are	you	usually	at school in the mornings?
Where	is	he	always	in the evenings?

3. Following is the pattern for information questions with other verbs:

information word(s)	auxiliary	subject	adverb	base form	balance of sentence
How much	do	you	usually	pay	for milk?
What kind of food	does	she	always	serve	at her parties?
How often	does	the earth		revolve?	

22   present participles

Besides the base form and -*s* form, another form of a verb is a PRESENT PARTICIPLE, or what is commonly referred to as an -ING FORM. Following are general rules for spelling present participles:

a. Ordinarily, only -*ing* need be added to a base form to make a present participle:

do, doing   bring, bringing   feel, feeling

b. When a base form ends in silent e, drop the e and add -ing:

drive, driving   take, taking   change, changing   live, living

c. If a one-syllable base form ends in -ie, drop the -ie and add -y before adding -ing:

lie, lying   tie, tying   die, dying

d. If a base form ends in -y, keep the -y and add -ing:

fly, flying   cry, crying   carry, carrying

stay, staying   copy, copying   play, playing

e. When a base form ends with a single consonant preceded by a single **stressed** vowel, double the final consonant before adding -ing:

begin, beginning   get, getting   knit, knitting   run, running

brag, bragging   hit, hitting   quiz, quizzing   stop, stopping

f. Do not double the -t in the verb *benefit* before adding -ing; the vowel preceding the -t is not stressed:

benefit, benefiting

23   the present continuous tense

1. We form the present continuous tense with the verb *be* as an auxiliary and a present participle as the main verb of a verb phrase. The adverb *not* is inserted between the auxiliary and the present participle in a negative verb phrase.

	singular	*plural*
1st person	I am (not) doing	we
2nd person	you are (not) doing	you } are (not) doing
3rd person	he	they
	she } is (not) doing	
	it	

2. The PRESENT CONTINUOUS TENSE is used to express:

a. An event that is taking place or happening now:

You *are now reading* about the present continuous tense.

b. An event that is taking place temporarily:

We're *living* in a hotel temporarily; we're *looking* for an apartment.

c. An event that is to take place in the near future:

> The ship *is sailing* at dawn.
> Our plane *is taking off* in a few minutes.

3. The adverbs *now, gradually, slowly, quickly,* and *rapidly* are some adverbs that occur with the present continuous tense. They are inserted between the auxiliary and the main verb:

> He *is slowly falling* in love with his neighbor's daughter.
> People *are now working* here in New York, but they're sleeping in Tokyo.

4. Usually, the frequency adverb *always* is used in the simple present tense to express the frequency of a habitual activity:

> My boss *always arrives* at the office at nine o'clock sharp. (exactly)
> Yes, boys and girls, the sun *always rises* in the East.

However, to **emphasize** the frequency of a habitual activity, *always* is used in the present continuous tense:

> Mailmen *are always worrying* about dogs.
> Healthy and happy children *are always playing*.

5. Some adverbial expressions which frequently occur with the present continuous tense are:

> He's not working *for the time being*. (temporarily)
> A lot of people in the world are starving to death *right now*. (at this moment)
> Yes, you're right; things aren't getting any cheaper *these days*. (now)
> Fortunately, the patient is getting better *little by little*. (gradually)

24   contrasting verb tenses

1. Words called ACTION VERBS may appear in either the simple present tense or the present continuous tense, but the meaning is different. Compare:

> He's *living* in Paris. (now or temporarily)   He *lives* in Paris. (fact)
> The sun *is setting*. (now)   The sun *sets* every day. (fact)

Following are some action verbs:

ask	gather	jump	make	repeat	tax
cook	get	kill	murder	rise	teach
develop	heal	laugh	operate	run	travel
do	help	leave	organize	save	work

2. Words called NONACTION VERBS almost always occur only in the simple present tense:

> I *am* a student.   This *costs* a lot.   I *love* you.

However, when we wish to express a temporary feeling, anger, or surprise, we use certain nonaction verbs in the present continuous tense:

> I *am* a man. (*but* I *am being* a man and going to the police about this matter.)
> I *love* you. (*but* I *am loving* these wonderful moments with you.)

Following are some nonaction verbs:

> admire   appreciate   cost   hate   look
> appear   be   feel   have   love

3. The nonaction verb *be* may also be used as a main verb in the present continuous tense when the verb is followed by an adjective:

> The children *are being* good today.
> You're *being* difficult, Sir.

4. To show possession, the nonaction verb *have* is most often used with the simple present tense:

> The elephant *has* a long trunk, but a relatively short tail.
> Their baby *has* blue eyes, very red hair, and a sweet little nose.

However, the verb occurs idiomatically with certain nouns in the present continuous tense:

> The mechanic is having *difficulty* fixing our car.
> Our club is always having *parties, dances, barbecues* (cookouts), *contests,* and even *lotteries.*
> Our son is having a tennis *lesson* today.
> I'm having nothing but *problems* with my boss.
> Fortunately, we aren't having much *rain* or *snow* this winter, nor are we having many *storms* or *blizzards.*
> We're having a wonderful (terrible) *time* on this vacation.
> Are you having *trouble* with any of the people at work?

25 yes - no questions

1. Yes–no questions in the present continuous tense are formed by inserting the subject of a sentence between the auxiliary and the main verb:

> *Is your brother having* a good time at school?
> *Are you doing* anything special at work today?

2. Adverbs follow the subject:

> Is *your mother always* practicing the piano?
> Are *you really* feeling good today?

3. Only the auxiliary (never the verb) appears in yes–no answers:

> Are your neighbors fixing up their house? Yes, they *are*. No, they *aren't*.
> Are you living here for the time being? Yes, I *am*. No, I'*m not*.

26 information questions

In information questions in the present continuous tense, the subject also follows the auxiliary in the verb phrase:

> Where *are your friends* staying in the city?
> What *are you* always doing at work these days?

27 adjective phrases; *the*

1. An ADJECTIVE PHRASE consists of a preposition and a noun with or without modifiers and is used to modify a noun. Unlike adjectives, adjective phrases follow the noun that they modify:

> The wine *in this glass* is bitter.   The clothes *in that closet* are mine.

2. The noun which the phrase modifies is often preceded by *the,* the DEFINITE ARTICLE. Like *a(an), the* is also called a determiner.

> *The fish* in the bag is spoiled.   *The sheep* on our farm produce good wool.

3. The verb in a sentence containing an adjective phrase must agree in person with the noun that is the subject of the sentence.

> The *cost* of these antiques *is* high.
> All the *people* in this room *are* good friends of mine.

4. When *the* precedes a word that begins with a vowel sound, it rhymes with *tea, see,* or *fee:*

> Prince Charles is *the heir* to the throne.
> For the size of its body, *the elephant* has a relatively small brain.

5. "X article" occurs before an uncountable or plural noun when the noun describes some thing or things *in general:*

X Air is composed of many different kinds of gases.
X Butter is very high in cholesterol.
X Oranges are good for you.

However, *the* appears with an uncountable or plural noun when the noun describes some thing or things *in particular:*

Unfortunately, *the air* in our town is quite polluted.
The butter in this package is rancid.
The oranges in this fruit salad are delicious.

28 neither, not one, both, and none

1. *Neither* + *of* + noun or pronoun takes a verb in the third person singular:

Neither of our dogs *barks* at strangers, and neither of them *chases* mailmen.

Pronunciation note: *Neither* may be pronounced in two ways: (a) the *nei* is pronounced so that it rhymes with *pie, buy,* or *lie;* (b) the *nei* sounds like *knee* and rhymes with *sea* or *pea.*

2. *Not one* + *of* + noun or pronoun also takes a singular verb:

What wonderful children! Not one of them *is* ever naughty.
Not one of my neighbor's children ever *sends* her a Mother's Day card.

3. *Both* + *of* + noun or pronoun always takes a plural verb:

Both of my children *are* good students; both of them *study* hard.

4. When *none of* precedes an uncountable noun, the verb is always singular:

None of this food *is* fresh.   None of his work *is* finished.

5. According to strict grammar rules, *none of,* because it means *not one,* should take a singular verb:

None of the students in the class *studies* as hard as you do.
None of his acquaintances *knows* much about his private life.

However, in informal usage, particularly in conversation, *none of* is frequently treated as plural:

None of my neighbors *gossip (gossips).*
None of the fellows on my team *practice (practices)* as much as I do.

29 compound pronouns and adverbs; *else* and *besides*

1a. COMPOUND PRONOUNS refer to indefinite persons or things, or indefinite quantities. They are:

	-body	*-one*	*-thing*
some-	somebody	someone	something
any-	anybody	anyone	anything
no-	nobody	no one	nothing
every-	everybody	everyone	everything

b. Compound pronouns may serve as subjects in a sentence:

Someone has my pen.
Nothing happens on Sunday.

or as objects:

We know *someone* in Tibet.
We know *nothing* about the recent scandal.

c. Compound pronouns always take a singular verb:

Everyone *needs* love and affection.
No one *has* the key to the house.

d. Compounds with *any-* do not ordinarily occur as subjects except in certain cases with the modal auxiliary *can*:

Anyone can enter this club.
Anything can happen to us on our trip.

e. Compounds with *some-* occur in affirmative statements and questions:

I have *something* for you.
Do you know *someone* in this town?

f. A negative verb phrase may follow compounds with *some-* when the compound is the subject of a sentence:

Someone (*somebody*) *doesn't have* a dictionary.
Something isn't working right.

g. Compounds with *any-* appear as objects in negative (never in affirmative) statements and questions:

I'm not doing *anything* special today.
Do you know *anyone* in Brazil?

2. COMPOUND ADVERBS like *somewhere, anywhere, everywhere,* and *nowhere* act as modifiers of verbs:

She's an oil specialist; she's living *somewhere* in the Middle East.

No one is living *anywhere* out in the middle of the desert.

They're going *nowhere* this weekend, but we're going *everywhere*.

3. The adjective *else* and the adverb *besides* frequently appear together with compound pronouns. Both *else* and *besides* mean *in addition to:*

Someone *else besides* (in addition to) you is wrong in this matter.

Do you want anything *else* today, Madam? Is there anything *else?*

What *else, besides* money and fame, do you want in your life, Miss?

4. Speakers and writers often confuse the adverb *besides* with the preposition *beside.* *Besides* means *in addition to,* but *beside* means *next to:*

She is always *beside* (next to) her husband in time of trouble.

The little boy is always *beside* his mother and holding on to her apron strings.

5. Compound pronouns always take a singular verb; however, in yes–no answers made in response to yes–no questions with *everyone,* we may observe a formal or informal style. Compare:

Is *everyone* coming to class tomorrow?

formal: Yes, *he* is.   *informal:* Yes, *they* are.

No, *he* isn't.   No, *they* aren't.

Does *everyone* have a dictionary?

formal: Yes, *he* does.   *informal:* Yes, *they* do.

No, *he* doesn't.   No, *they* don't.

6. We may also observe a formal or informal style when a pronoun refers back to *everyone.* Compare:

formal: Everyone in the room is going to give me *his* homework to-morrow.

informal: Everyone in the room is going to give me *their* homework tomorrow.

Note: The informal style is never acceptable in formal writing, and strict grammarians strongly object to its use in either formal or informal writing and speaking.

7. When speaking to a mixed group of men and women together, we refer back to *everyone* with *his or her:*

Does *everyone* in the audience have *his or her* program for this evening?

Everyone in this group has *his or her* own personal problems to deal with.

30 prepositions of time

1. We use *on* with a day of the week:

   He and his father always go to the mosque together *on Fridays*.

2. *In* is used with the name of a month:

   In Nepal, the monsoon usually comes *in June* and stays for three months.

3. A month plus a date requires *on*:

   Where are you going to be *on January 1, 2000?*

4. An hour of the day always takes *at*:

   Our plane is taking off *at 12 o'clock* sharp.

5. A year is accompanied by *in*:

   Does the new millennium begin *in the year 2000 or 2001?*

6. Noon and midnight require *at*:

   The execution of the rebels is *at noon*.
   At the seance, the medium's message is arriving *at midnight*.

7. *Dusk* and *dawn* also require *at*:

   How beautiful our valley becomes *at dusk!*
   How lonely and deserted this town looks *at dawn!*

8. *Night* is always preceded by *at*:

   How exciting and busy New York City is *at night!*

9. *The night* combines with *in*:

   Oh! What joys and sorrows there are *in the night!*

   Note: *In the night* rarely occurs in conversation or in general writing. The expression has the added connotation of darkness and danger, perhaps in the poetic sense.

10. *In* also combines with *the morning* (*the afternoon, the evening*):

    Do you prefer to go to school *in the morning*, *in the afternoon*, or *in the evening?*

11. We use *during* to express duration:

    Children, we're playing inside today *during* the rain.

12. *In* or *during* occurs with a part of the day (week, month, year, season) that is considered a period of time having duration:

> The birds in the north fly on their annual trip south *in/during the fall.*
> I usually have one or two cups of coffee *in/during the morning.*

13. *From* is used to express the beginning point of a period of time, and we use *to* for expressing the end point:

> We're going to be traveling on the train *from eight o'clock* tomorrow morning *to ten o'clock* tomorrow night.
> Everyone in the class is going to be studying hard *from the beginning to the end* of the semester.

31 prepositions of direction

1. We *arrive at* an office, airport, hotel, or similar type of place:

> We're *arriving at* the Plaza Hotel at around eight o'clock.
> Our train *arrived at* Grand Central Terminal at noon.

Usually, we *arrive in* a city:

> Excuse me, Captain, when do we *arrive in* Bangkok?
> Our train was delayed by a flood, so we *arrived in* Calcutta ten hours late.

However, we sometimes use *arrive at* for cities, particularly when we are traveling over great distances and we expect to continue traveling on:

> We *arrived at* Singapore a half hour late, laid over (waited) for an hour, and then took off for Sydney.
> We finally *arrived at* Kathmandu after thirty-three days of trekking.

2. Idiomatically, *get to* may substitute for *arrive in* (*at*):

> We're *getting to* (*arriving in*) Rangoon at midnight.
> Don't worry; we're *getting to* (*arriving at*) the station a little late, but we're not missing our train.

3. *Get into* is an idiomatic substitute for *enter*:

> Just how difficult is it to *get into* (*enter*) Harvard University?
> He and his wife are trying to *get into* (*enter*) the most exclusive club in town.

Get out of is a substitute for *leave*:

> What time are you *getting out of* (*leaving*) the office today?
> "*Get out of* (*leave*) my life," she said to him in great anger.

4. We can *pass, travel, fly, go, come, walk,* or *run through* a place, and we can also do all these things *to* or *from* a place.

5. We can also go, *come, walk, climb, crawl, run,* or *fly up* or *down.*

6. *Toward*(s) occurs with *move, walk, drive, sail,* or *run,* and often with the verb *head:*

> My horse is running faster; he knows we're *heading toward* home.
> Our ship is *heading toward* the Equator; it will soon be very hot.

7. Idiomatically, *to be through with* can mean *to be finished with:*

> Are you *through* (*finished*) with that big job for your boss?

To get through can mean *to finish:*

> What time are you going *to get through* (*finish*) at the office today?

8. The idiomatic expression *on time* means at an exact time:

> Try to get to class *on time* (at nine o'clock) every morning, class.

In time means before a specific time:

> Try to get to class tomorrow *in time* (before nine o'clock) to speak to me before the class begins.

32   expressing future time with the present continuous tense

1. The present continuous tense is often used to express future time. When this occurs, future time expressions like *next week, tomorrow,* or *in an hour* (day, week, etc.) usually appear in the sentence:

> I must get to work; the boss *is coming* back in a minute.
> A lot of things *are happening* in our town next weekend.

2. When a time expression is not used, the adverb *soon* is frequently employed:

> Everyone in my office *is soon getting* a promotion and a big raise.
> Children, Christmas and Santa Claus *are coming soon*, so be good.

33   expressing duration in the future; *(for) how long, probably, at least,* and *until*

1. Besides expressing a single event in future time, the present continuous tense is used to express the duration of an event in future time:

ESL GRAMMAR HANDBOOK 39

Tomorrow, I'm *studying* from early in the morning to late at night.
The present recession *is lasting* longer than the last one.

2. (*For*) *how long* usually occurs in information questions asking for the duration of an event. *For* is optional; it is used for emphasis.

(*For*) *how long* are you and the children playing on the beach today?
(*For*) *how long* is this meeting probably lasting?

3. The adverb *probably* usually follows the auxiliary:

We're *probably* staying at this hotel for another week or so.

In negative verb phrases, *probably* may precede or follow the auxiliary:

This movie (probably) is *probably* not lasting a long time.
We *probably* aren't staying a long time. We're *probably* not staying a long time.

4. The preposition *for* is optional in statements about duration in future time:

My wife, children, and I are staying at the beach (*for*) three weeks.
My brother and I are camping up in the mountains (*for*) a whole month this summer.

5. The expression *at least* (meaning *the minimum of*), which usually follows *for*, is employed when we are not certain of the length of the duration:

We're shopping downtown today (for) *at least* the whole afternoon.
My husband and I are keeping our old car (for) *at least* another year.

At most (*the maximum of*), the opposite of *at least*, occurs most often at the end of a statement:

My wife and I are staying with my mother-in-law for three days *at most*.
I'm working at this company for another year *at most*.

6. Expressions of time introduced by the preposition *until* are often used to express how long the duration of an event is going to be:

I'm staying here in the basement *until the end of the hurricane*.
He loves this firm (company); he's probably working here *until the end of his business career*.

34   "X prepositions"

1. Students of the language frequently put a preposition where there should be none. We refer to "no preposition" as "X preposition."

2. "X preposition" occurs with the noun *home* and action verbs like *get, arrive, go,* etc.:

> Would you like to go *X home* now, Elizabeth?
> We aren't getting *X home* in time to watch our favorite program on TV.

3. The verb *enter* requires "X preposition":

> He's planning to *enter X* the navy when he gets out of high school.
> Are you *entering X* the university this summer or in the fall?

However, the words *enter into* occur with the nouns *argument, discussion,* and *debate:*

> I don't want to *enter into* an *argument,* a *discussion,* or a *debate* with anyone in my class.

4. When we are referring to schools, clubs, and organizations which require an application for entrance, *get into* may be used as an idiomatic substitute for *enter:*

> How does one *get into* (enter) the best club (school, band) in town?

5. In reference to rooms, buildings, parks, etc., we use the verb *enter* (rarely *get into*):

> They *entered X* the room (building, park) in a great hurry.

6. "X preposition" occurs with the verb *leave:*

> When are you *leaving X* Rome? (you are in Rome and planning to leave)

For also occurs with the verb:

> When are you *leaving for* Rome? (you are not in Rome but plan to go)

7. The verb *visit* requires "X preposition":

> I would like to *visit X* the Grand Canyon when I go to Arizona.

But with the expression *to pay a visit,* we must use the preposition *to:*

> When I go to Washington, I'd like to *pay a visit to* the White House.

8. The verb *reach* takes "X preposition" when it means *to arrive at a destination:*

> Our caravan *reached X* the oasis in the middle of a sandstorm.

We use *reach for,* however, when the verb means *to attempt to grasp:*

> He *reached for* his glasses, but they were too far away for him to get.

9. "X preposition" occurs with *attend:*

They're devout Christians and *attend* X church every Sunday.

However, the two-word verb *attend to* means *take care of* or *look after:*

Sir, you must *attend to* this important matter at once.

10. "X preposition" occurs with the adjective *near:*

Fortunately, or unfortunately, our house is *near* X the police station. (but *close to, next to, far from*)

35 *be going to* + a base form

1. *Be going to* + a base form is also used for an event in future time:

The new millennium *is going to begin* (is beginning) soon.

2. We form negative verb phrases by inserting *not* between *be* and *going to:*

The student rebels *are not going to release* the hostages soon.

3. *To go* in a verb phrase may be omitted:

We are not going (to go) to school today; it's a holiday.
I'm not going (to go) away during my vacation; I'm going to stay home.

4. We frequently use *be going to* to express duration in the future:

We**'re going to be** on this ship *for at least two weeks;* it's a long trip.
Our group **is going to stay** in Warsaw *for three days at most.*
How much longer **are** you **going to study** English?

36 *be going to* + *be* + a present participle

Statements with *be going to* + *be* + a present participle are used for emphasizing the continuing nature (duration) of an event:

We're *going to be studying* a lot of new things in the next few months.
The monsoon is over; it's *not going to be raining* for the rest of the summer.

Pronunciation note: When we are speaking quickly, *going to* may sound somewhat like "gonna":

We're *"gonna"* have a happy marriage; we love each other very much.

This contraction does not occur when we are speaking slowly.

37 *too, very,* and *enough*

1. Both the adverbs *too* and *very* are called INTENSIFIERS, but they are completely different in meaning. *Very* intensifies (makes stronger) the word that it modifies:

> The world is *very large,* and we want to see all of it.

Too intensifies the word that it modifies, but beyond a point that is desirable:

> The world is *too small* for its population; we must have family planning.

2. *Too* suggests impossibility or something that we cannot do or do not like:

> This candy is *too sweet.* (I really don't want to eat it.)
> This coffee is *too hot.* (I don't think I can drink it.)

Very suggests possibility, something that we can do, or like very much:

> This candy is *very sweet.* (May I have some more, please? It's delicious.)
> This coffee is *very hot.* (I'd like more, please; it tastes good.)

3. When *too* precedes an adjective or adverb, the phrase is almost always followed by an infinitive:

> This candy is *too sweet to eat.*
> This coffee is *too hot to drink.*

For + a noun or pronoun may precede the infinitive, but its use is optional:

> This candy is too sweet (*for me*) to eat.
> This coffee is too hot (*for John*) to drink.
> The thief is running too fast (*for the police*) to catch.

4. Sometimes *very* is followed by an adjective + an infinitive, but the meaning is that of possibility rather than impossibility. Compare:

> *possibility:* It's *very difficult for him to do* this work, but he does it well.
> *impossibility:* It's *too difficult for him to do;* he can't do it.

5. The adverb of degree *enough* means possibility when it follows an adjective (never an adverb) and is followed by an infinitive:

> This project is *easy enough* (for a child) *to do.*
> Our dining table is *large enough* (for us) *to seat* eight people comfortably.

6. *Enough* always follows the adjective that it modifies:

Our daughter isn't *old enough* to wear lipstick; she's only twelve.

However, when *enough* is used to modify a noun, it may precede or follow the word:

Someday, there isn't going to be *enough oil* (*oil enough*) for everyone. We don't have enough wood (*wood enough*) to build a fire.

38 regular and irregular past forms; spelling and pronunciation

1. In the simple past tense, regular verbs end in *-ed* in all persons.

	singular		*plural*	
1st person	I		we	
2nd person	you	landed	you	landed
3rd person	he she it		they	

2. Here are the rules for spelling regular past forms:

a. The past tense form of a regular verb can usually be formed by simply adding *-ed* to a base form:

fail, failed   work, worked   <u>itch, itched</u>

b. When a regular verb ends in *-e,* add only *-d:*

love, loved   place, placed   tape, taped

c. When a regular verb ends in *-y* preceded by a consonant, change the *-y* to *-i* and add *-ed:*

try, tried   busy, busied   pry, pried

d. For regular verbs ending in *-y* preceded by a vowel, a change is not made; add only *-ed:*

play, played   pray, prayed   stay, stayed

e. When a regular verb ends with a single consonant preceded by a single **stressed** vowel, double the consonant before adding the *-ed:*

drip, dripped   slam, slammed   omit, omitted   quiz, quizzed

The commonly used irregular verbs are listed in Appendix 3 of *ESL Grammar Quiz Book.*

Pronunciation Note: When a base form ends in a *t* or *d* sound, the final syllable in the past form of regular verbs is pronounced. Practice pronouncing the following past forms.

-ted		*-ded*	
benefited	corrected	attended	landed
collected	reported	decided	needed
permitted	started	ended	recorded
expected	waited	graded	reminded

When base forms that end in -k, -p, -f, -gh, -s, -ce, -sh, -ch, and -x become -ed past forms, they end with a *t* sound.

-k	*-p*	*-f*	*-gh*	*-s*
asked	stopped	puffed	coughed	passed
looked	helped	cuffed	roughed	tossed
liked	dropped	stuffed	laughed	bossed
locked	hoped	bluffed		crossed

-ce	*-sh*	*-ch*	*-x*
practiced	pushed	scratched	taxed
danced	flushed	itched	fixed
produced	crushed	hatched	boxed
enticed	mashed	touched	mixed

All past forms except for those described above end with a *d* sound:

died   owed   received   figured   called   prepared

39   the simple past tense

1. The SIMPLE PAST TENSE is used for an event that occurred at a definite point of time in the past:

The United States *declared* its independence from Great Britain on July 4, 1776.
The American Civil War *began* in 1860 and *ended* in 1865.

2. *Was* and *were* are the two forms in the simple past tense of the verb *be*. No contractions of *was* and *were* occur with subject pronouns.

	singular	*plural*	
1st person	I was	we	
2nd person	you were	you	were
3rd person	he	they	
	she } was		
	it		

World War I *was* a training ground for the Second World War.

The Vikings *were* the first Europeans to come to the New World.

3. In the negative form of the verb *be* in the simple past tense, the adverb *not* follows the verb. *Wasn't* and *weren't* are the contractions of *was not* and *were not:*

> I *wasn't* at school yesterday, and my parents *weren't* at work; it was a holiday.

4. For all verbs in the simple past tense other than *be*, the negative is formed with the auxiliary *did*, the past form of *do*, followed by *not*, followed by the base form. *Didn't*, the contraction of *did not*, occurs in informal usage.

	singular		*plural*	
1st person	I		we	
2nd person	you	} did not (didn't) work	you	} did not (didn't) work
3rd person	he		they	
	she			
	it			

40   adverbs with the simple past tense

1. Usually, frequency adverbs follow the verb *be* in affirmative phrases:

> They *were always* very happy during their marriage.
> He *was usually* a very good boy when he was little.

For emphasis, the adverb is sometimes put before the verb:

> He *sometimes was* busy, but only once in a great while.
> My grandparents *never were* religious, but they believed in God.

2. If the verb is *be,* adverbs follow *not* in negative verb phrases:

Fortunately, our daughter *wasn't ever* sick when she was little.
Our boy *wasn't always* on the baseball field when he was younger, but he was most of the time.

3. With all verbs except *be,* frequency adverbs always precede the verb. If the phrase is negative, the adverb precedes the base verb, not the auxiliary:

They *never got* along well during their marriage; it lasted only a year.
He *usually shaved* only once a week during his vacation in the mountains.
My grandfather didn't *ever smoke* a cigar, but he smoked a pipe.

41   yes-no questions in the simple past tense

1. In yes–no questions, *was* or *were* is placed before the subject of a sentence:

Were you at the graduation ball?
Was yesterday your birthday?

Adverbs are placed after the subject:

Was *she ever* absent from school during that time?
Were *you always* a good student then?

2. Expletive *there* follows the verb:

Was there an earthquake last night?
Was there any fun in your life then?

3. In short yes–no answers, we most often use *wasn't* or *weren't* in *no* answers.

Yes, {
I was.
you were.
he (she, it) was.
we (you, they) were.
}

No, {
I wasn't.
you weren't.
he (she, it) wasn't.
we (you, they) weren't.
}

4. For emphasis, we use the noncontracted form; the stress is on *not.*

Were you somewhere in the bank during the robbery? No, I was *not.*
No, we were *not.*

5. Expletive *there* precedes the verb in yes–no answers:

Was there a good reason for your mistake? Yes, *there was.* No, *there wasn't.*

6. Except for the verb *be,* the auxiliary *did* is used with all verbs in yes–no questions:

auxiliary	subject	verb	balance of sentence
Did	Napoleon	die	a happy man?
Did	you	do	any favors for him?

Pronunciation note: *Did you* often sounds like *did-jew.*

7. *Did* also appears in short yes–no answers.

Yes, $\begin{Bmatrix} \text{I} \\ \text{you} \\ \text{he (she, it)} \end{Bmatrix}$ did. No, $\begin{Bmatrix} \text{we} \\ \text{you} \\ \text{they} \end{Bmatrix}$ didn't (did not).

42 information questions in the simple past tense

1. Information questions with the verb *be* have the following pattern:

information word	verb	subject	adverb	balance of sentence
Where	were	you		yesterday?
How	was	the movie		last night?
Where	were	they	usually	during the evenings?

2. Information questions with all other verbs have the following pattern:

information word	auxiliary	subject	adverb	verb	balance of sentence
What	did	you		do	last night?
How much	did	he		pay	for his new car?
What	did	you	usually	do	on your vacation?
Where	did	she	always	sleep	at her grand-mother's?

43 *who, whom,* and *whose* in information questions

1. The interrogative pronoun *who* occurs as the subject of an information question: for example, in *John lives in this town, who* replaces *John,* the subject of the sentence:

Who lives in this town?

2. When an information word is the subject of a question, the usual question form is not observed:

> *Who* in this class speaks Russian? (*but* What language does Boris speak?)
> *Who* is living in Johannesburg? (*but* Where is your brother living?)
> *Who* came to America first? (*but* When did Columbus come to America?)

3. In the simple present tense, the verb following *who* is usually in the third person singular:

> *Who is* knocking at the door?
> *Who* in this class *has* a car?

4. A subject and an auxiliary occur in short responses to questions with *who:*

> *Who* runs the political show in Washington, D.C.? *The President does.*
> *Who* in the class is transferring to another school? *I'm not.*
> *Who* assassinated Abraham Lincoln? *John Wilkes Booth did.*
> *Who* was at the front door? *The mailman was.*

5. *Whom* is the object form of *who;* it may be used as the object of a verb:

> *Whom* (object) do you know in Stockholm? I know nobody (object).
> *Whom* (object) do you love? I love *my wife* (object).

or as the object of a preposition:

> *With whom* does your brother live? He lives *with a classmate.*
> *For whom* are the bells tolling? They're tolling *for the nation's war dead.*
> *To whom* did you hand the message? I handed the message *to the Ambassador.*

6. *Whose* is the possessive form of *who* and usually precedes a noun:

> *Whose jacket* is John wearing? He's wearing *Fred's jacket.*
> *Whose money* did you spend? I spent *my money.*
> *Whose car* does your wife drive to work? She drives *her car.*

However, *whose* may appear alone when the noun is understood:

> *Whose* is John wearing? He's wearing *Fred's.*
> *Whose* did you spend? I spent *mine.*
> *Whose* does your wife drive to work? She drives *hers.*

44   postponed prepositions

1. In formal usage, a preposition precedes *whom* in an information question:

> *To whom* are you addressing the letter?
> *With whom* did he fly?

In informal usage, *who* replaces *whom,* and the preposition appears at the end of a question. A preposition in this position is called a POSTPONED PREPOSITION.

> *Who* are you addressing the letter *to?*
> *Who* did he fly *with?*

2. Postponed prepositions also occur in questions with *whose:*

> Whose pen are you writing *with?*
> *Whose* desk are you working *at?*

3. When they occur, postponed prepositions are sometimes followed by an adverb of time or a prepositional phrase:

> Who are you working *for now?*
> Dear, who is your father speaking *to on the phone?*
> Who do you usually sit *with in your English class?*

4. Postponed prepositions also occur with *what:*

> *What* are you talking *about?*
> *What* pot are you cooking the spinach *in?*

45   information questions; formal versus informal usage

Reminder: Today, *whom* rarely appears in information questions in informal speech. Compare:

> *formal: With whom* is your roommate in love?
> *informal and more common: Who* is your roommate in love *with?*
> *formal: With whom* are you going to the party?
> *informal and more common: Who* are you going to the party *with?*

46   information questions; information words as subjects

Reminder: When an information word is the subject of a question, the usual question form is not observed. Compare:

What happened in 1939? . . . *World War II* began. (*but* When did the war begin?)
Who lives at the North Pole? . . . *Santa Claus* does. (*but* Where does Santa Claus live?)

47   pronoun substitutes; *one, some; what* and *which*

1. As we have discussed, pronoun substitutes are used to avoid unnecessary repetition:

What interesting *paintings!* Do you like *them?*
This lesson is difficult. Do you understand *it?*

2. *One* or *ones* often occurs as a substitute for countable nouns:

These are delicious *chocolates.* Would you like *one?*
We have three sizes of *apples.* I'd like a dozen of the large *ones,* please.

Some or *any* substitutes for uncountable nouns:

What wonderful *cheese* this is! Would you care for *some?*
Would you like wine with your cheese? No, thank you, I don't care for *any.*

3. The information word *which* is frequently used in questions with *one*(s). When our choice is small, we use *one:*

There are a German and French film playing in town tonight. *Which* (*one*) would you like to see?

Ones follows *which* when our choice is larger:

Look at all these nice bathing suits. *Which* (*ones*) do you like best?

However, *one* follows *which* in sentences containing a singular verb:

What nice hats! *Which one* **is** best for me?
How beautiful these bracelets are! Which *one* **is** best for my wrist?

4. *One* also occurs as a subject in statements or questions. When this occurs, *one* means *you in general:*

Children, *one* does not put one's elbow on the table at dinner.
Does *one* wear shoes in a Hindu's house?

In American English, *you* (meaning *one* or *you in general*) occurs in speech more frequently than *one:*

Do *you* (does one) have nice weather in your hometown? Yes, *we* do.
Do *you* (does one) need a ticket to get into the stadium? No, *you* don't.

5. *Which* may refer to persons or things:

> *Which person* do you wish to speak to? *Which classroom* is his?
> *Which woman* in this office is your boss? *Which desk* is hers?

What usually occurs with only things:

> *What classroom* do you use every day? *What desk* do you usually
> sit at?

6. We use *which* when there is a choice of only a few things or persons
(usually two, perhaps three or four):

> *Which camera* do you want to use, the new one or the old one?
> *Which neighbor* has a new car, the one next door or the one across the
> street?

What is generally used when there is a choice of many things:

> *What* is your name? (there are thousands of names)
> *What* is your address in Los Angeles? (there are many addresses in Los
> Angeles)

7. Frequently, however, *which* and *what* are interchangeable:

> Which (what) bus are you taking? (*Which* suggests a choice of a few
> buses, *what* suggests a choice of many.)

48   compound subjects and objects

1. The COORDINATE CONJUNCTIONS *and, but,* and *so* are also called CON-
NECTIVES because they connect a word with another word, a phrase with a
phrase, or a clause with another clause.

2. Grammatical units like nouns and pronouns which are joined
together by a coordinate conjunction are called COMPOUND; for example, a
COMPOUND SUBJECT may be two pronouns:

> *She and I* are in love.
> *He and I* went all the way through school together.

or two nouns:

> *Panthers and tigers* live in this jungle.
> *Cats and dogs* are natural enemies.

or a noun and a pronoun:

> *My neighbor and I* never see each other.
> *He and his dog* go hunting together a lot.

3. In a compound subject with the pronoun *I,* it is customary for the pronoun to follow the other word:

> *My roommate and I* have a good relationship.
> *She and I* get along quite well.

Other pronouns come first when combined with a noun:

> *She and her sister* are identical twins.
> *He and his girlfriend* are engaged.

4. COMPOUND OBJECTS occur as the object of a verb:

> My mother loves *my sister and me* a great deal.
> I saw *her and her husband* at the circus last night.

or of a preposition:

> I played cards with *my neighbor and her boyfriend* all night long.
> I dreamed about *you and a lot of other people* last night.

5. The object pronoun *me* usually follows the other word in a compound object:

> You forgot to send an invitation to *my mother and me.*
> Don't tell a soul; keep this information a secret between *you and me.*

Other object pronouns come first in a compound object:

> Yes, I often see Tom; I just had dinner with *him and his wife* two nights ago.
> Yes, we know Dick and Jane very well; we went with *them and their children* on a vacation last summer.

> **Note:** Frequently, students (and native speakers) mistakenly put a subject pronoun in a compound object. Compare:

correct	***incorrect***
This is a secret between you and me.	This is a secret between you and [I].
The President knows my wife and me well.	The President knows my wife and [I] well.

6. When two items appear in a compound, we do not use a comma:

> *Trees and flowers* surround their school.
> *Flies and mosquitoes* infest their house.

When three or more items are coordinated, commas are used to separate the items; however, a comma before the conjunction preceding the last item is optional:

All my *aunts, uncles*(,) and *cousins* came to my last birthday party.
Movies, television, newspapers(,) and *radio* fill all my free time.

7. A list of three or more items is called a COORDINATE SERIES. The series can be listed in a random order:

We'd like *a radio, a sofa, a kitchen chair,* and *a new rug* for the hall.
I need *an eraser, a few pencils, some ink, a ruler,* and *a good fountain pen.*

or the order may be fixed as in certain common phrases:

Ladies and Gentlemen	men, women, and children	ham and eggs
chicken and rice	tall, dark, and handsome	the birds, the
meat and potatoes	safe and sound	bees, and
		the flowers

However, we must often arrange the items in some kind of logical order.

a. Less important to more important (three items or more):

the secretary, the First Lady, and the President
the stool, the chair, the table, and the bed

b. More important to less important (three items or more):

the King, the Queen, and the Prince
the President, the Vice-President, the Secretary of State, and the Secretary of Defense

c. More important to less important (two items always take this order):

pens and pencils   paper and ink   love and money

d. Smaller to bigger:

the flute, the guitar, the cello, and the piano

e. Earlier to later:

the morning, the afternoon, and the evening
morning coffee, lunch, afternoon tea, cocktails, and dinner

49 compound verbs

1. In COMPOUND VERBS, objects, adverbs, and prepositional phrases are often present in the compound:

He *exercises in the gym **and** jogs* in the park every afternoon.
He *works hard **and** makes* a lot of money.
She *doesn't speak **and** write* English as well as she understands it.
The ship *hit an iceberg **and** sank* within a few hours.

2. The coordinate conjunction *or* frequently occurs in negative compound verb phrases:

> She *doesn't knit, sew,* **or** *darn.*
> My roommate *doesn't smoke, eat* sweets, **or** *drink* alcohol.

Or can be used in affirmative sentences also:

> He *sings* **or** *dances* (I'm not sure which).
> I will *succeed* **or** *die* trying.

3. A compound verb in the present continuous tense has only one auxiliary:

> The children **are** always *laughing and playing.*
> I**'m** *going* to the store *and buying* some food for the weekend.

50 compound infinitives

Objects, adverbs, and prepositional phrases may also occur in COMPOUND INFINITIVES. *To* in the second infinitive is omitted:

> I'd like *to meet* my favorite movie star *and* **get** his autograph.
> We'd like *to work* in the city *and* **live** in the country.
> He's willing *to work* hard *and* **produce** for the company.

51 compound adjectives and adverbs

COMPOUND ADJECTIVES AND ADVERBS frequently occur:

> How *quickly and inexpensively* that company operates!
> What a *hot and humid* night it is!
> How *fast and hard* he always works and plays!

52 compound sentences with semicolons; *too* and *either*

1. A SIMPLE SENTENCE always contains a subject and a verb.

subject	*verb*	*balance of sentence*
Hermits	often live	in caves.
Life	is changing	fast in my town.
We	voted	for the loser in the election.

2. When two simple sentences are closely related to each other, they may be combined to form a COMPOUND SENTENCE. One way the two sentences can be joined together is with a SEMICOLON (;):

> Money goes fast. We need to make more. = *Money goes fast; we need to make more.*
> She's a poet. Her poetry is famous. = *She's a poet; her poetry is famous.*

When two sentences appear together in a compound sentence, each sentence is called a MAIN CLAUSE (independent clause).

3. The adverb *too*, preceded by a comma, frequently occurs in the second main clause when the verb phrase in the first main clause is affirmative:

> That young man *is* a genius; his father is one, *too.*
> She's a very fickle person; her boyfriend is quite fickle, *too.*

4. The adverb *either*, also preceded by a comma, may appear in the second main clause when the verb phrase in the first main clause is negative:

> Our apple tree *never bears* any fruit; our pear tree doesn't ever bear any, *either.*

or when a negative word occurs as the subject in the first clause:

> *None* of his friends at school smokes; he doesn't smoke, *either.*

> **Pronunciation note:** *Either* may be pronounced so that it rhymes with *beaver* or *cleaver*, which is most customary in the United States. Or it may be pronounced so that the first syllable rhymes with *pie, sky,* or *I,* which is most common in the United Kingdom.

53 compound sentences with *and* and *but; miss*

1. Two main clauses may be joined together by the coordinate conjunction *and* to form a compound sentence:

> Our village is high up in the mountains, *and* we are surrounded by beautiful views.

2. When the two main clauses are short, we do not ordinarily use a comma:

She's coming and I'm going.
The water is high and the fish are running.

Since main clauses are usually longer than those in the examples above, a comma is most often placed between the two clauses to avoid confusion. In speech, a pause separates the two clauses:

The sun is setting (pause), and the mosquitoes are coming out.

Note: Generally, a comma in writing indicates there is a pause in speech.

3. The coordinate conjunction *but* may also connect two main clauses. A compound sentence with *but* shows a positive-negative contrast:

He's a very nice person, but he has almost no friends.
They seldom do any work, but they always have money in their pockets.

4. A comma usually precedes *but,* except when the two clauses are short:

The days on the desert are dry and hot, *but* the nights are always cool.
He's poor but he's happy. They're rich but they're unhappy.

5. A *but* clause is called a CLAUSE OF UNEXPECTED RESULT when the result expressed in the second clause is unexpected (a surprise), or not logical according to the situation expressed in the first clause:

She's the worst student in the class, *but she always gets the highest scores.*

6. *Miss,* besides being a title for an unmarried woman (*Miss Brooks*), is also used as a verb; there are several meanings:

a. To fail to hit, reach, attain, or catch:

You *missed* the target.
The catcher *missed* the ball.

b. To fail to attend or perform:

He *misses* class all the time.
She never *misses* a day of work.

c. To omit or leave out:

The teacher *missed* a few names on the list.
Don't *miss* any questions.

d. To be absent from:

I have found my wallet, but the money is *missing.*
When I opened my suitcase, some things were *missing.*

e. To feel loss or unhappiness:

He's homesick; he *misses* his home and family.
All my grandfather's old friends are gone; he *misses* the old days.

Note: *Miss, Mr.,* and *Mrs.* are always capitalized. Because *Mr.* and *Mrs.* are abbreviations (Mister, Mistress), they always take a period. *Miss* is not an abbreviation and never takes a period. *Ms.,* a relatively new title for either a married or an unmarried woman, takes a period even though it is not an abbreviation.

54 compound sentences with *so*

When *so* is used to introduce a main clause, it is called a CLAUSE OF EXPECTED RESULT because the result is expected and logical according to the situation expressed in the first main clause:

She's intelligent and clever, *so she's doing well at school.*
He's a very selfish person, *so he has few friends.*

55 abridged infinitives

1. We may in some cases abridge (abbreviate) an infinitive by omitting the base form because it is understood. ABRIDGED INFINITIVES occur most often in the main clauses of contrast introduced by *but:*

My neighbor across the street wants to move, *but his wife doesn't want to* (move).
She'd like to eat out tonight, *but her husband wouldn't like to* (eat out).

2 These abridgements can occur with the verbs *like, want, need, would like,* and *prefer:*

My grandmother works very hard, but she doesn't *need to.*
He doesn't like to eat dinner early, but his wife *prefers to.*

3. Abridged infinitives can also occur with the expression *don't care* (meaning *don't want*):

I'd like to go on a hike today, but my friends *don't care to.*
My roommate wants to watch TV, but I *don't care to.*

4. We sometimes need to insert an object between the verb and the word *to* when we refer to the subject in the first clause:

John Doe is running in the next presidential election, but his family doesn't *want him to.*
The cat is eating the dog's food, but I don't *want it to.*
The children are watching TV all the time, but I don't *want them to.*

5. Students frequently forget to use the *to* in an abridged infinitive. Compare:

correct	*incorrect*
I need to work today, but I don't want *to*.	I need to work today, but I don't want [X].
He wouldn't like to go, but I'd like *to*.	He wouldn't like to go, but I'd like [X].

56 *too, either, so, neither, and,* and *but*

1. To avoid repetition, we may abridge the second main clause in a compound sentence through SUBSTITUTION.

2. An auxiliary can represent the omitted words in a clause of contrast:

Our neighbors don't have a house pet, but we *do*.
She's always working, but her husband *isn't*.

3. An auxiliary plus the adverb *too* can substitute for a second main clause with an affirmative verb:

An elephant is large, and a hippopotamus *is too*.
My niece sent me a birthday card, and my nephew *did too*.

4. The adverb *so* plus an auxiliary may also act as an affirmative substitute. When this occurs, the subject is inverted and follows the auxiliary:

Cats and dogs are always fighting, and *so are* my neighbor and his wife.
My girlfriend went to the movies with me, and *so did* her younger sister.

Note: *So* (as an adverb) in this pattern has the meaning of *also; so* (as a coordinate conjunction) has the meaning of *therefore*.

5. An auxiliary plus *not* plus *either* may occur as a substitute for a second main clause with a negative verb:

His grandfather isn't living, and his grandmother *isn't either*.
The Republicans didn't have a good candidate, and the Democrats *didn't either*.

6. *Either* may follow an auxiliary in the affirmative when the subject of the abridged second main clause contains a negative word:

> Jackie never jogs, and *none* of her friends *does either.*
> I don't like to pay taxes, and *not* many others *do* either.

7. *Neither* plus an auxiliary also occurs as a negative substitute. As with *so,* the subject is inverted and follows the auxiliary:

> No one in my family smokes, and *neither does* anyone in yours.
> The South does not want war, and *neither does* the North.

57 complex sentences; *when, before,* and *after*

1. Unlike a main clause, a SUBORDINATE CLAUSE (dependent clause) cannot stand alone as a sentence; it must always accompany a main clause either expressed or understood. For example, the subordinate clause *when I go home* means nothing when it occurs by itself; however, the clause does have meaning when joined with a main clause:

> When I go home, *I always walk through the park.*

A sentence containing both a main and subordinate clause is called a COMPLEX SENTENCE.

2. There are three kinds of subordinate clauses:

> **a.** Adverbial clause: *If I were a millionaire,* I would live like one.
> **b.** Adjective clause: He *who laughs last* laughs best. (old saying)
> **c.** Noun clause: We know *what the teacher's secret is.*

3. A TIME CLAUSE is one kind of an adverbial clause. Such clauses are introduced in a sentence by INTRODUCTORY WORDS (clause markers) like *when, before,* and *after:*

> He always showers *before he shaves.*
> Grandpa usually smokes a pipe *after he has dinner.*
> We always slept late every morning *when we were on our vacation.*

4. Usually, a complex sentence contains two, three, or perhaps four clauses. The three basic positions of a complex sentence are:

initial position	*mid position*	*final position*
We always go for a walk	after we have breakfast	when the weather is nice.

5. We do not use a comma when an adverbial clause occurs in the final position of a sentence:

> No one was at the station to meet us X *when our train arrived.*
> We want to cut down that tree X *before it falls down and hurts some-one.*

6. In American written English, when an adverbial clause appears in initial position, a comma usually follows:

> *When my father takes a shower or bath,* he always sings a lot.
> *After I woke up this morning,* I felt like a million dollars.
> *Before I go to bed,* I almost never forget to set my alarm.

When the two clauses are short, however, we need not use a comma:

> When it's hot I swim a lot. When it's cold I skate and ski.

7. A verb phrase in the simple present tense after *when, before,* and *after* can express future time:

> How old are you going to be *when we enter the new millennium?*
> *When the good weather comes,* we're going to go hiking in the mountains.
> I'm going to be in the classroom *before the bell rings tomorrow.*
> Let's take a break *after we do the next quiz.*

8. When both the main and time clauses are in the simple present tense to express an occasional or habitual activity, frequency adverbs often appear in the main clause:

> Grandma *usually snores* a lot when she *takes* her afternoon nap.
> After I *get up* in the mornings, I *hardly ever go* back to bed.
> Before the children *go* to sleep, I *always tell* them a story.

58 *while*

1. When *while* occurs in a time clause, we are emphasizing the duration of two events taking place now or in the future:

> Ladies and Gentlemen, while the juggler *is standing* on his head, he *is going to be juggling* a dozen oranges.

2. When the subordinate conjunction *while* appears in a complex sentence, both the main and time clauses can contain the simple present tense or its continuous form:

While she's *taking* (*takes*) care of the baby, she's *trying* (*tries*) to do her homework.

or the main clause may contain a future form:

While she's putting the children to bed, her husband *is going to be doing* (*will be doing*) the dinner dishes.

59   complex sentences; *though, even though,* and *although*

1. The subordinate conjunctions *though, even though,* and *although* have the same meaning and are used to introduce adverbial CLAUSES OF CONCESSION. Such clauses are always accompanied by main clauses of unexpected result:

Though a fox is small, it's a very clever animal.
Our garden is flourishing *even though we don't use any fertilizer.*
Although he is an ambassador, he never has any money to spend.

2. *Although* is more formal than *though* and *even though.* Because of the presence of the intensifier *even,* *even though* has the strongest sense of concession of the three conjunctions.

3. *Though* and *although* most frequently occur in the initial position of a sentence:

Though our house was right in the middle of a hurricane, there was very little damage, fortunately.
Although she's a royal princess, she doesn't have a penny to her name.

4. *Even though* often occurs in the final position of a sentence:

My neighbor down the street is always talking about politics *even though he doesn't know much about it.*
She doesn't have a foreign accent *even though she isn't a native speaker.*

Punctuation reminder: When an adverbial clause occurs in initial position, a comma usually follows:

Young man, although you are the son of a very rich man, you mustn't waste your money on foolish and useless things. Money doesn't grow on trees. (old saying)

60 complex sentences; *as soon as* and *until*

1. The subordinate conjunction *as soon as* in an adverbial time clause expresses an event that happens just before another event occurs:

> I'm going to wake up *as soon as* the sun rises; the light will wake me up.
> The world will be a better place *as soon as* someone finds a good and cheap substitute for oil.

2. In addition to the introductory words *when, before, after,* and *as soon as*, the subordinate conjunction *until* is used as an introductory word (clause marker) in an adverbial time clause. *Until* indicates the duration of an event or nonevent:

> She's going to stay with this company *until she becomes the president of the firm.*
> We're going to stay up in the mountains *until the first snow of winter falls.*

3 When a time clause is introduced by *until*, the verb in the main clause is often in its negative form:

> George, you're *not going to be* a successful salesman until you find something better to sell.
> The strikers *aren't going* back to work until they get a better deal.

or there is a negative word in the subject:

> *Not* one of us in the office is going to be happy until the company pays us more money and gives us better benefits.
> *None* of us is going to be happy until our team wins the championship.

The verb in the time clause is almost always in the affirmative:

> No social life is going to take place in his life until he *finishes* his project.
> I'm not going to apologize to them until they *apologize* to me.

4. Students sometimes confuse a time clause with a time phrase. A time phrase never contains a subject or a verb; a time clause always does. Compare:

time phrase	*time clause*
. . . until the end of the journey.	. . . until *the journey comes* to an end.
. . . after the game.	. . . after *the game ends.*

Punctuation reminder: When an adverbial clause occurs in initial position, a comma usually follows:

Until they move into a larger apartment, they're not going to have any children.

As soon as the bell rings, the children are going to go out and play.

Note: *Till* has the same meaning as *until*; however, it occurs most frequently in speaking.

He's not going to be satisfied *till* he gets a perfect score.

61   complex sentences; *because* and *since*

1. The subordinate conjunction *because* is used as an introductory word in a CLAUSE OF REASON:

They're getting a divorce *because his pets don't get along with hers*.

A clause of reason answers *why*:

Why are you sleeping outside on the porch tonight?
. . . *because our airconditioner isn't working*.

2. Clauses of reason introduced by *because* usually occur in final position:

She never has any financial problems *because she's an heiress*.

For emphasis, they sometimes appear in initial position:

Because we have so much inflation now, our money doesn't go very far.

3. The subordinate conjunction *since* may also be used to introduce a clause of reason answering *why*. Such clauses almost always take the initial position:

Since he doesn't have any sense, he's always getting into trouble.
Since we're in the middle of an economic boom, our company is doing very well.

Note: *Since* also occurs in time phrases or clauses, usually in conjunction with main clauses containing verb phrases in the present perfect tense:

We have lived in this country *since 1980*.
She has been a student *since she came to this country two years ago*.

4. The adverbial phrases *because of* and *due to* also introduce phrases answering *why*; such phrases most often appear in initial position followed by a comma:

Because of the very hot weather, our children are going swimming a lot.

Due to the high rate of unemployment, many people are moving out of our town.

Punctuation reminder: When an adverbial clause occurs in initial position, a comma usually follows:

Because the workers are on strike, our company's production is at a standstill.

Since our neighbors have triplets, there are always a lot of diapers on their clothes line.

62   negative information questions; *why*

1. In formal usage, in negative questions, the adverb *not* follows the subject:

Why do *the rich not* help the poor?
Am *I not* your father, Son?

In informal usage, the adverb *not,* contracted with the verb *be* or other auxiliary verbs, precedes the subject. *Why* is the usual information word that occurs in negative information questions.

Isn't it a beautiful day?
Why *don't you* want to go for a walk in the park?
Didn't you have a good time in Europe?
Why *wouldn't you* like to go there again?

Pronunciation note: (a) *aren't you* sounds like *arn-chew;* (b) *don't you* sounds like *don't-chew;* (c) *weren't you* sounds like *weren't-chew;* (d) *didn't you* sounds like *didn't-chew;* and (e) *wouldn't you* sounds like *wooden-chew.*

2. In informal usage, *aren't I* replaces the rather formal *am I not:*

formal: Am *I not* the King? My word must be obeyed.
informal: Aren't *I* a good friend of yours? Tell me what's wrong.

Note: *Ain't,* meaning "am not, is not, are not, has not, and have not," does not occur in educated speech and writing.

3. When we ask a negative yes–no question, we usually expect our listener to agree with us; we are just making small talk (conversation):

Don't you like this place? *Indeed I do—I love it.*
Didn't you enjoy the party? *Of course I did—I was with you.*

A negative yes–no question can also express surprise:

> Really, don't you love your mother and father? I can't believe it.
> Aren't you feeling well? You look as healthy as *ever*.

4. Negative information questions with *why* may express irritation:

> Why don't those mosquitoes go away?
> Why aren't I making more money?

or a great deal of anger:

> "Why don't you get out of this house and never come back?"
> "Why don't you shut up?" she shouted.

A negative information question with *why* may also take the form of a polite request or suggestion:

> Why don't we go out to dinner tonight? Would you like to?
> Why don't you take off your coat, sit down, and relax for a few minutes?

To be courteous, and perhaps more persuasive, we insert the polite word *please* between the subject and the verb:

> Billy and Paula, why don't *you please take* your elbows off the table?
> Mr. Jones, why don't *you please sign* this contract now? You don't want to miss this golden opportunity, do you?

5. On occasion, when we are making polite requests with negative questions with *why,* the verb *be* may occur with *don't:*

> Mr. Rogers, why don't you *be* on time once in a while?
> Children, why don't you please *be* quiet?

63 the emphatic form of the simple present tense; conjunctive adverbs, *however*

1. Adverbs used as connectives to join two main clauses in a compound sentence are called conjunctive adverbs (transition words). Some commonly used conjunctive adverbs are:

accordingly	consequently	moreover	otherwise
afterward	furthermore	nevertheless	then
besides	however	nonetheless	therefore

2. When the clauses of a compound sentence are linked by a conjunctive adverb, a semicolon is put between them, and a comma usually follows the adverb:

I'm taking my umbrella with me; *otherwise*, I am going to get wet.
The man was insane when he wrote the will; *therefore*, the will is invalid.
We're not getting our supplies; *consequently*, our company is losing money.

3. *However,* which is similar in meaning to *but,* occurs most often in formal usage:

The dam project is going to cost a great deal; *however*, it's going to improve agriculture in our area.
She's losing her beauty as she gets older; *however*, she's becoming wiser.

We use a comma to separate *however* from the balance of a sentence when the adverb appears in initial or final position:

She's a nice person. *However*, she has no friends. She has no friends, *however*.

It is separated by two commas when the adverb is within a sentence:

It was difficult for her to make up her mind. She finally decided, *however*, to give all her money to charity.

4. Ordinarily, when we are speaking and writing in the simple present tense, we do not use any auxiliaries in affirmative verb phrases:

They *have* a beautiful house.   He *plays* checkers well.

For expressing strong emphasis, however, we use the EMPHATIC FORM of the simple present tense, which is made by combining *do* or *does* with a base form:

My neighbors don't have a car, but they *do have* a beautiful house.
Your brother doesn't play chess, but he *does play* checkers very well.

The frequency adverbs *often* and *sometimes* may appear between the auxiliary and the base form:

She never goes to the ballet, but she *does often go* to the opera.
He seldom does anything around the house; however, he *does sometimes mow* the front lawn.

5. The emphatic form most often occurs in clauses introduced by *but* or *however:*

They don't have much money in the bank, but they *do have* a great deal of gold in their safe deposit box.
He doesn't speak Chinese well; however, he *does speak* Japanese fluently.

It may also occur in one of a pair of main clauses coordinated by *but* or *however:*

> Yes, I *do love* you, but I don't love you as much as I do someone else.
> Yes, she *does have* beautiful looks; however, she doesn't have much of a personality, does she?

6. In speech, the stress is usually on the auxiliary:

> Yes, I *do* like this city, but I certainly don't love it as some people do.

64 the emphatic form of the simple past tense

We use *did* as the auxiliary in the emphatic form of the simple past tense.

> She said nothing when he insulted her, but she *did walk* away from him.
> We rarely had potatoes when we were in China; however, we *did eat* a lot of rice.
> Yes, we *did enjoy* our dinner last night, but we both got indigestion.

65 negative openings

1. When a sentence begins with a NEGATIVE OPENING (a negative word or a word that has a negative connotation), the emphatic form is used. A form of the verb *be* or an auxiliary + a subject follows the negative opening.

> *Never does the weather* change much this time of year.
> *Seldom is London* as warm as it is today.
> *Rarely did we* go to Paris while we were in France last summer.

2. The adverb *not* combined with *once, often,* or *ever* may occur as a negative opening:

> *Not often* does my bus come on time, but it comes sooner or later.
> *Not once* did I get a perfect score last week.
> *Not ever* was she nervous during the climb to the summit of Mt. Everest.

3. The adverb *only* combined with certain adverbial expressions may also occur as a negative opening:

> *Only once a day* (week, month, year) does his roommate take a bath.
> *Only once in a while* (on occasion, from time to time) do they argue.
> *Only for the time being* are we staying in this terrible town.

Only also combines with prepositional phrases to make a negative opening:

> *Only for the love of money* does that person work.
> *Only at my school* does one find such good teachers.

4. The coordinate conjunction *nor* is sometimes used in rather formal usage to connect two main clauses. As *nor* makes a negative opening, we must use the emphatic form in the second main clause:

> I'm not tired now, *nor am I* thirsty or hungry.
> He's not working now, *nor does his roommate* have a job.
> We never went to Melbourne when we were in Australia, *nor did we* go to Perth—we visited only Sydney.

Frequency adverbs often occur in such sentences with *nor;* they follow the subject:

> He never arrives at the office early, nor does *he ever* leave late.
> They don't usually go to concerts, nor do *they often* go to the ballet.
> She never seems busy, nor does *her boss ever* seem to have anything to do.

66   tag questions

1. When we ask a simple yes–no question, we do not ordinarily know the answer until the person to whom we are speaking has given his or her reply:

> "Are you in love with me?" he asked. "No, I'm not," she replied.

With a *tag question,* however, we most often know the answer, or we are just seeking confirmation or making conversation:

> "You're in love with me, aren't you?" he asked with a smile. "Of course I am; you know I love you very much."

2. The first part of a tag question is a statement—for example, *The world is a small place*—and the second part of the question is called a *tag ending:*

> The world is a small place, *isn't it?*

In writing, a comma separates the statement from the tag ending; in speech, a pause occurs:

> Life is getting more and more expensive, (pause) isn't it?

3. To form a tag ending, we use a form of the verb *be* or another auxiliary verb, along with a pronoun substituting for the noun subject. When a statement is positive, a negative tag ending follows:

The Republican candidate for office *would like* to lower taxes, *wouldn't she?*

Life *seems* to go by faster the older one gets, *doesn't it?*

There's quite a bit of rain in your part of the country, *isn't there?*

The government *made* quite a few mistakes last year, *didn't it?*

When a statement is negative, the tag ending is affirmative:

John *wouldn't like* to pass up this opportunity, *would he?*

These oranges *aren't* as sweet as those, *are they?*

You *didn't take care of* that situation, *did you?*

There isn't enough time in a day, *is there?*

4. When *never, rarely,* and *seldom* occur in a statement, the tag ending is positive:

Those people *rarely* do anyone a favor, *do they?*

You'd *never* like to live in this city for good (forever), *would you?*

The teacher *seldom* chews gum in class, *does he?*

5. Either a formal or informal style may be observed in tag endings:

formal: I am the president of this company, *am I not?*

informal: I'm going to see you later at the game, *aren't I?*

formal: The President of the nation speaks for the people, *does he not?*

informal: Bob Brown plays better than anyone else on the team, *doesn't he?*

Note: Chiefly British: He has a car, *hasn't he?* They've time, *haven't they?*

6. When we ask a tag question and we are certain of the answer (which is almost always), the final intonation of the tag ending is down:

You love me, *don't you?* You didn't lie to me, *did you?*

When we are *not* certain of the reply (which is unusual), the intonation is up:

You love me, *don't you?* You didn't lie to me, *did you?*

67 the imperative mood; titles

1. The IMPERATIVE MOOD is used for making requests or commands. The verb always appears as a base form.

Close the door on your way out.

Mind your own business.

It is also used for giving instructions:

> Cook the turkey for six hours.
> Boil the potatoes for twenty minutes.

2. The polite word *please* is frequently (and best) used in a command or request at the beginning of a sentence:

> *Please* make yourself comfortable; my house is your house. (old Spanish saying)

If the sentence is short, it may be placed at the end, preceded by a comma:

> Make yourself at home, *please.*
> Move over, *please.*

3. In a command, the subject of a sentence (always the second person singular or plural) does not appear but is understood:

> (You) Open your book, please.
> (You) Return to your starting places, please.

4. In negative commands or requests, *do not* (*don't*) precedes the verb.

> *Don't touch* that wet paint, please.
> Please *do not pry* into my affairs.

Frequency adverbs may precede the verb in a command:

> *Always tell* the truth, *never tell* a lie, and don't *ever cheat* at school.

5. To make a command more imperative, we sometimes use the emphatic form:

> *Do do* your homework, please.
> Please *do tell* me about your adventure last night.

6a. A person's name or title may appear at the beginning of a sentence:

> *Your Honor*, please don't put me in jail.
> *John*, please don't make me do something that I don't want to do.

If the command is short, the name or title may appear at the end:

> Please believe me, *Sir.*
> Knock him out, *Rockie.*
> Don't arrest me, *Officer.*

Note: *Mister* is not used as a title (except in *very* informal usage):

> Please give me a dollar, *Sir* (never *Mister*).
>> *Sir* often appears as *sir.*

b. *Miss* is a title for an unmarried woman:

> *Miss*, please watch out; the streets in this part of town are dangerous at night.

c. *Madam* is a title of courtesy used alone as a form of address for any woman:

Madam, please remove your hat in the theater.

Madam may be prefixed to a title indicating rank or office:

Madam President   Madam Ambassador   Madam Secretary

Ma'am, the abbreviation of *Madam*, occurs most frequently in conversation:

Yes, *Ma'am*, you're the boss. No, *Ma'am*, you're not in my way.

d. Mrs. is not used as a title:

Madam (or *Miss* or *Ma'am*; never *Mrs.*), please be seated at the head of the table.

But we use *Mrs.* with a surname, or in the fixed phrase *Mr.* and *Mrs.* + a surname:

Mrs. Taylor, please tell me about your career in the business world.
Mr. and Mrs. Crawford, please accept our heartfelt congratulations on your golden anniversary.

e. *Ms.* + a surname does not ordinarily occur in speaking, only in writing.

f. Usually, *lady* is not used as a title:

Madam (or *Miss* or *Ma'am*; never *lady*), your slip is showing.

Lady may be used as a feminine title of nobility and other rank (most common in the United Kingdom and the British Commonwealth):

Lady Godiva   Lady Mountbatten   Lady Guinevere

or in *very* informal English:

Hey, *lady*, need a ride? Hey, *lady*, where did you learn how to drive?

Ladies may occur as a title when we are addressing a group of women:

Ladies, now is the time to fight for equal rights for all.

g. *Gentleman* is never used as a title:

Sir (never *gentleman*), please keep off the grass.

But *Gentlemen* occurs as a title when we are speaking to a group of men:

Gentlemen, now is the time for revolutionary changes in our society.

Or in the fixed phrase *Ladies and Gentlemen*:

Ladies and Gentlemen, please lend me your ears for a few minutes.

h. *Madame* is the French title of courtesy for a married woman; it is more formal than the English *Mrs.* + a surname. *Madame* may be used by itself (alone) or with a surname:

> *Madame*, please try on this gown.
> *Madame Arnal*, please try out this fragrance.

Madame is also prefixed to the names of famous women of high rank or distinction:

> *Madame Curie   Madame Chiang Kai-shek   Madame Callas*

i. *Judge, Doctor,* and *Professor* are commonly used titles:

> *Judge,* don't put me behind bars, please.
> *Doctor,* please take care of your health.
> *Professor,* tell us the reasons for the French Revolution.

In elementary school, children may occasionally address a teacher as *Teacher:*

> *Teacher,* please read the story of *Cinderella* to us.

However, adults never address a teacher as *Teacher:*

> *Sir* (or *Professor, Miss, Madam, Ma'am, Madame, Mr. Smith, Mrs. Jones, Bob,* or *Alice,* but never *Teacher*), please don't give us any homework tonight.

68 *let's;* polite requests with *shall* and *would*

1. Let's (let + us) may precede a verb in the imperative mood:

> *Let's go* out tonight and have a good time. *Let's get* out of the house.

Not follows *let's* in the negative form:

> *Let's not* worry about the future too much. *Let's not* waste our time.

2. In very informal usage, *let's don't* may occur before the verb:

> *Let's don't get* home late.
> *Let's don't fight,* Buddy.

On occasion, the expression *don't let's* is used:

> *Don't let's* kid around.
> *Don't let's* get excited, Boss. *Don't let's* hurry.

3. Let's or *let's not* may be the response to a request or suggestion with *let's:*

> Let's stay home tonight. *Let's.* (It's too cold to go out.)
> Let's walk to school today. *Let's not.* (It's too far to walk.)

Let's do or *let's don't* occurs in less formal usage:

> Let's go around the world. *Let's do.* (We need a change.)
> Let's buy a big car. *Let's don't.* (Gas is too expensive now.)

4. *Shall I* or *shall we* means *do you want me (us) to* when it precedes a verb in the imperative mood; in a way we are asking for *permission:*

> *Shall I* (do you want *me* to) set the table for you?
> *Shall we* (do you want *us* to) take a picnic lunch to the park today?

> **Note:** Second person (you) does not occur in polite requests with *shall.*

5. *Please do* or *please don't* is the most common response to a question with *shall I.*

> *Shall I* continue with my story? *Please do,* Tom; it's fascinating.
> *Shall I* tell this story to your roommate? *Please don't,* Jim; it's none of his business.

Let's or *let's not* is the usual response to *shall we:*

> *Shall we* dance? *Let's;* it's my favorite record. (*sometimes* let's do)
> *Shall we* play another game? *Let's not;* I'm exhausted. (*sometimes* let's don't)

6. *Shall we* occurs with *let's* in tag questions:

> Let's stop in Rio on our way to Buenos Aires, *shall we?*
> Let's go to Puerto Rico by ship, *shall we?*

Or shall we occurs with *let's not:*

> Let's not have more children, *or shall we?* Aren't two enough?
> Let's not stay home this evening, *or shall we?* Don't you think it's too cold to go out tonight?

7. *Shall I* or *shall I not* may occur when one is faced with a dilemma:

> *Shall I or shall I not* ask that man to marry me? Please don't, Jane; he's not the right man for you.
> *Shall I or shall I not* quit my job? Please do, Frank; that boss of yours is driving you crazy.

Shall we or shall we not occurs when two or more people are faced with a dilemma:

> *Shall we or shall we not* go to the police about this problem? Let's not, dear; our neighbor's dog will eventually stop barking.
> *Shall we or shall we not* attack at dawn? Let's, Sir; our troops are ready to fight.

8. *Would you* (*please*) may also precede a verb in the imperative mood:

Would you please repeat that question more slowly.
Pluto, *would you* get out of the kitchen, please.

Punctuation note: Since polite requests with *would you* are not questions, it is customary to use a period at the end of the request:

Would you please sit down. (*but* Would you like to sit down?)

9. *Would you* + (*please*) + *not* also occurs before a verb in the imperative degree, and it makes for a very strong request:

Danny, *would you please not* tease your baby sister; you're making her cry.
Mr. Smith, *would you please not* put your garbage on my front lawn.
Terry, *would you please not* talk about me behind my back; I don't like it.

Pronunciation reminder: *Would you* usually sounds like *wood-jew.*

69 reflexive pronouns

1. As a mirror reflects an image of ourselves, a REFLEXIVE PRONOUN refers back to the subject of a sentence; for example, in *He's always looking at himself in the mirror,* the reflexive pronoun *himself* refers back to *he,* the subject of the sentence.

	singular	*plural*
1st person	myself	ourselves
2nd person	yourself	yourselves
3rd person	herself	themselves
	himself	
	itself	

2. A reflexive pronoun always occurs as an object and frequently the object of a preposition:

She's angry *at herself.* He no longer believes *in himself.*
They're always talking *about themselves.* I sometimes talk *to myself.*

3. Reflexive pronouns may function as the direct object of certain verbs:

He *burned himself* seriously in a kitchen accident.
I *cut myself* when I was shaving with a dull razor blade.

Freddy, when you cheat at school, you're just *cheating yourself.*
They always *enjoy themselves* when they go on their vacations.
My neighbor *hurt himself* seriously while he was fixing his car.
At the rate he smokes, he's slowly *killing himself.*
To love others, we must *love ourselves.*
My roommate always *pushes herself* to do well in everything she does.
My watch is old, but it's automatic; it *winds itself.*

4. In rather formal usage, a reflexive pronoun is sometimes used to intensify a pronoun or noun:

No one but *the President himself* can make such an important decision as this.
The *job itself* is not so bad, but I don't like my boss, and the salary is poor.
We ourselves are responsible for what we do in our lives.

5. Idiomatically, a reflexive pronoun preceded by the preposition *by* means *alone:*

Actors and dancers are always working among people, but painters and writers most often work *by themselves* (alone).
No, no one helped us on this project; we did it *by ourselves* (alone).

Note: Students sometimes confuse the idiom *by oneself* (alone) with the emphatic use of reflexive pronouns; for example, in *The director **himself** made the decision,* we are only emphasizing the subject (perhaps the director made the decision in a room crowded with people); however, in *The director made the decision **by himself** in the other room,* the suggestion is that the director was alone when he made the decision.

70 direct and indirect objects

1. A noun (or pronoun) that is the DIRECT OBJECT of a verb usually answers the questions *What?* or *Whom?*:

What did they buy yesterday? They bought *a house.*
Whom did you see at the gym? I saw *them.*

2. A noun or pronoun that is the INDIRECT OBJECT of a verb answers the questions *To whom?* or *For whom?* When it is in a prepositional phrase, it follows the direct object.

To whom did he offer the bribe? He offered the bribe *to the police.*
For whom did she make a birthday cake? She made a birthday cake *for me.*

3. Some verbs followed by direct object + prepositional phrase with *to* are:

>bring   hand   offer   pay   send   teach   write
>
>give   lend   owe   sell   take   tell

4. Some verbs followed by direct object + prepositional phrase with *for* are:

>bake   buy   draw   get   make
>
>build   cook   find   knit   reserve

5. An indirect object may precede a direct object. When this occurs, we omit the *to* or *for* of the prepositional phrase:

>She frequently writes letters *to me.* = She frequently writes *me* letters.
>I baked an apple pie *for my neighbor.* = I baked *my neighbor* an apple pie.

6. Reflexive pronouns may function as the indirect object of a verb:

>Did you send a package *to yourself?* (= Did you send *yourself* a package?)
>I'm going to reserve a room *for myself.* (= I'm going to reserve *myself* a room.)

71   separable versus inseparable multiple-word verbs

1. A verb may be joined with a preposition to make a TWO-WORD VERB; the preposition in such a verb is referred to as a PARTICLE:

>I *picked out* a brown tie for my father and a blue one for my uncle.
>They were living in Tehran when the Islamic Revolution *broke out.*

2. There are two kinds of two-word verbs, SEPARABLE and INSEPARABLE.

    a. In a separable verb-preposition combination, the particle may occur before or after a noun object:

>The baby ate *up his food* = The baby ate *his food up.*
>They're calling *out my name* = They're calling *my name out.*

    b. Time expressions and prepositional phrases always remain in final position, whether the two-word verb is separated or not.

>He called up his friend *yesterday* = He called his friend up *yesterday.*
>I put away the dishes *in the cupboard* = I put the dishes away *in the cupboard.*

c. If the object is a pronoun, it is always inserted between the separable verb and the particle:

> These are beautiful pearls. Why don't you *try them on*, Madam?
> What a nice 10-speed bicycle this is! Shall I *try it out?*

3. In inseparable verb-preposition combinations, a noun or pronoun object always follows the particle; an inseparable verb is never separated:

> Would you please *look after my children.* (*never* look my children after)
> We'd like to call on him. (*never* call him on)

4. One- or two-word verbs that may take direct objects are called TRANSITIVE, and verbs that may not take direct objects are called INTRANSITIVE. Sometimes, a two-word verb may be either transitive or intransitive, but the meaning of the verb changes. Compare:

> *transitive:* The terrorists *blew up* the factory. (caused the factory to explode)
> *intransitive:* The factory *blew up.* (exploded)
> *transitive:* Why don't you *take off* (remove) your jacket and stay awhile?
> *intransitive:* Our plane finally took off. (left the ground and ascended)

5. A second particle may be joined to a two-word verb to form a *multiple-word verb* (three-word verb):

> He doesn't *get along with* his landlord; he's moving out.
> She isn't going to *put up with* any nonsense from the children today.

6. A verb may also be combined with a noun + a particle to form a multiple-word verb:

> Why doesn't she like to *take care of* her house?
> Why don't you *take advantage of* this golden opportunity?

> **Note:** A list of commonly used multiple-word verbs and certain expressions will be found in Appendix 1 of *ESL Grammar Quiz Book.*

72 the past continuous tense

1. To form the PAST CONTINUOUS TENSE, *was* and *were* are used as auxiliaries, and a present participle serves as a main verb. *Not* is inserted between the auxiliary and the main verb in a negative verb phrase.

	singular	*plural*
1st person	I was (not) doing	we
2nd person	you were (not) doing	you } were (not) doing
3rd person	he } she } it } was (not) doing	they

2. Adverbs usually precede the main verb in the past continuous tense:

I *was finally falling* asleep when the phone suddenly rang.
He *was always fooling around* when he worked for that company.

3. In yes–no and information questions, the subject of a sentence follows the auxiliary:

Was he sleeping when you called him up?
How *were you* feeling when you woke up this morning?

4. The usual question form does not occur when an information word is the subject of a sentence:

Who was sitting in this room when you came in?
How many people were living in England at the time of Shakespeare?

5. One use of the past continuous tense is to emphasize the occurrence of an event that took place at a particular point in the past:

I *was sleeping* at the time of the earthquake; I didn't feel a thing.
Several women *were wearing* saris at the reception last night.

6. We also use the past continuous tense to emphasize the duration of an event that has a beginning and an end in past time:

The sun *was shining* from the beginning to the end of our summer vacation.
What a complainer he was! He *was complaining* from the day he was born to the day he died.

7. As with the present continuous tense, we use the adverb *always* with the past continuous tense to emphasize a habitual activity in past time:

I remember my grandfather *was always smoking* a cigar.
It *was always snowing* when we were at Lake Placid.

8. The past continuous tense occurs most frequently in the main clause of a complex sentence that has a time clause in the simple past tense:

I *was watching* television when the news about the assassination *came on.*

In effect, the past action that is expressed in the time clause interrupts the past continuing action expressed in the main clause:

> When we *got* to the class late (interruption), the teacher *was passing out* new material.

9a. The subordinate conjunction *while* may appear in a complex sentence in which both the main and time clauses contain the past continuous tense:

> While he *was speaking,* he *was chewing* gum 20 miles an hour.
> She *was nervously wringing* her hands while she *was talking* to me.

While emphasizes the duration of an event or the passage of time:

> While we *were traveling* around the world (during our trip), we *were sleeping* a lot in some very strange places.
> While the clown *was riding* on his donkey, he *was blowing* bubbles in the air.

b. *When,* however, is used for an event that takes place at a specific moment, or for an event that has no duration. Compare:

> *When* my mother *met* my father (at that moment), he was playing a piano.
> *While* the President and the First Lady *were greeting* the arriving guests (during that time), an orchestra was softly playing in the background.
> *When* he *hit* the other car (at that moment), he was driving 30 miles an hour.
> *While* the mugger *was hitting* the woman (during that time), she was screaming for the police.

10. The past continuous tense sometimes follows *when,* but we are emphasizing *time* when this occurs, not duration:

> When I was working for that company (from 1979 to 1981), I was making very little money.
> When it was raining (late this afternoon), all the laundry on the line got wet.

11. For expressing duration in the past, or emphasizing the occurrence of an event in the past, the simple past tense and the past continuous tense are essentially interchangeable; the past continuous tense only adds emphasis:

> Everything in the country changed (was changing) following the Revolution.
> While we lived (were living) in London, we never had a car; we didn't need one.

73   *be going to* + a base form in past time

1. When *be going to* + a base form is used for an event in past time, it means the event did not take place even though it had been planned; in other words, it was an unrealized plan. The form in past time most often occurs in complex sentences containing clauses of contrast introduced by *but*:

> They *were going to tear down* that beautiful cathedral, but the city government finally decided to save it from demolition.
> My neighbors *weren't going to move out of town*, but they finally decided to.

2. The adverb *instead* quite often appears in such sentences, usually in final position:

> What a tragic story! He was going to be one of the richest and most powerful men in the world, but he ended up in the gutter *instead.*
> The revolutionary government was going to build a new and better society, but they ended up with anarchy *instead.*

74   the simple future tense

1. To form the SIMPLE FUTURE TENSE, we use the modal auxiliary *will* (and *shall* in the first person) and a base form as the main verb in a verb phrase. *Not* is inserted between the auxiliary and the base form in negative verb phrases:

> We *shall defend* our rights. The people *will not tolerate* oppression.

Won't, the contraction of *will not,* occurs in informal usage:

> He says he's a good friend of mine, but he *won't* stand up for me in court.

	singular	*plural*
1st person	I will (shall) (not) do	we will (shall) (not) do
2nd person	you	you
3rd person	he she it	will (not) do	they	will (not) do

2. Today in modern American English, the use of *shall* in the first person is not common; *will* is most often used in all persons:

> I *will* not give up my position at that company.
> My *wife and I will* not put up with any backtalk from our children.
> They *will* put by a little money every month to save for a rainy day.

The use of *shall* (and *shan't,* the contraction of *shall not*) is chiefly British:

> *We shall* have a lovely time when we go up to Oxford for the weekend, *shan't we?*

A person in the United States would most likely say:

> *We will* have a nice time when we visit the University of Virginia, *won't we?*

However, *shall* occasionally appears in second and third person to express strong determination or inevitability:

> The judge looked at the convicted murderer and said, "*You shall* be hanged by the neck until dead."
> He's laughing now, but *he shall* regret his mistakes when he's older.

Shall also appears in polite requests with *shall I* or *shall we.*

> *Shall we or shall we not* take a break when we finish this quiz?
> I would like to cook dinner for the two of us. *Shall I?*

3. Contractions of *will* (*shall*) and subject pronouns are present in informal usage:

> *I'll* go back on my diet tomorrow.
> *She'll* call out your name in a few minutes.

$$
\left.\begin{array}{l} \text{I} \\ \text{you} \\ \text{he} \\ \text{she} \\ \text{it} \end{array}\right\} \text{'ll} \qquad \left.\begin{array}{l} \text{we} \\ \text{you} \\ \text{they} \end{array}\right\} \text{'ll}
$$

4. Adverbs usually precede a base form:

> I will *always respect* my parents.
> I'll *never break* my promise.
> You'll *eventually graduate* from this school, won't you?
> None of my friends will *ever reveal* this secret to anyone, and neither will I.

5. *Be going to* and *will* are essentially interchangeable:

> They *will* (*are going to*) move into their new house soon.
> We *won't ever* (*aren't ever going to*) make out in this business deal.

However, *will* gives much greater force to a statement. *Be going to* expresses only simple futurity and is used in connection with our ordinary everyday activities:

> I'm going to go to the butcher's.
> We're going to take the dog for a walk.

Beside simple futurity, *will* expresses:

a. Promise: "I'll never take a bribe while I'm in public office," the candidate promised.

b. Determination: I will protect my family and property with my life.

c. Inevitability: This world will eventually come to an end.

d. Prediction: "The world will come to an end in 1980," the prophet wrongly predicted.

6. *Will* is also used to give a strong directive or some critical instructions:

> Jason, you *will do* this work today; otherwise, you'll fall too far behind.
> You *will go* to the post office; there you *will buy* some stamps and mail these letters, and then you *will go* to the bank to deposit this money order.

7. *Will you please* (*would you please*) appears before a base form in more formal usage:

> Boys and girls, *will you please quiet down;* the bell has rung.
> Darling, *will you please marry* me.

8. For the very immediate future (almost right after we speak), *be about to* + a base form may occur:

> Hurry up! The show *is about to begin;* I want to see the opening number.
> You don't have a tissue, do you? I'm *about to sneeze.*
> Mr. Reynolds, I'm *about to get* angry; you'd better not say another word.

75   *probably*

1. Like other adverbs, *probably* precedes the base form in a verb phrase in the simple future tense:

> My grandparents will *probably move* to Arizona when they finally retire.

It sometimes precedes *will:*

> Yes, I *probably will* do this composition over.
> Perhaps; they *probably will* make up, and I hope they do.

2. *Always* and *eventually* may follow *probably will:*

> Yes, they *probably will always* live in this town for the rest of their lives.

Yes, I think so; we *probably will eventually* move from the city to the country.

Always may also follow *probably won't* (*will not*):

We *probably won't always* live in this house; it's really too large for us.
I *probably won't always* be single; I'll eventually find a mate.

Ever also occurs:

We *probably won't ever* be millionaires, but we'll always have each other.
She *probably won't ever be* a great pianist, but she'll eventually play well.

3. *Soon* may also follow *probably:*

The government forces will *probably soon* put down the revolutionaries.
We'll *probably soon* have dinner, children, so wash your hands and face.

4. In negative phrases, in formal usage, *probably* precedes *not:*

The committee will *probably not* announce a decision until there is a consensus.
There will *probably not* be elections in that country until there is a change in the government.

In informal usage, *probably* precedes *won't:*

We *probably won't* win this game; they're beating us.
I *probably won't* wake up early tomorrow morning; I'm completely worn out.

76 the future continuous tense

1. To form the FUTURE CONTINUOUS TENSE, we use *will* (*shall*) and the verb *be* as auxiliaries and a present participle as the main verb of a verb phrase. *Not* follows *will* in negative verb phrases.

	singular	*plural*
1st person	I will (shall) (not) be doing	We will (shall) (not) be doing
2nd person	you	you
3rd person	he she it } will (not) be doing	they } will (not) be doing

2. Adverbs are usually inserted between *will* and *be*, the two auxiliaries:

> He'll *always be looking* for new financial opportunities; he loves money.
> The class *will probably be doing* a lot of quizzes next week.
> It's late September; the birds *will soon be* flying south.

3. *Soon* may appear at the end of a verb phrase or in the final position of a sentence:

> *Soon*, our enemy will be giving up.
> They'll be loading up the plane *soon*.

Probably and *soon* may occur together:

> You'll *probably soon* be getting through with this work, so be patient.

or they may be separated by *will*:

> The professor *probably will soon* be passing out the final grades.

4. *Probably* may precede or follow *will*:

> We *probably will* be running into a lot of old friends at the cocktail party.
> We *will probably* be setting off for our camp in the mountains soon.
> They *probably will* not be seeing us off at the airport.
> I *will probably* not be throwing away these papers; they're too important.

5. We use the future continuous tense to emphasize the occurrence of an event at a definite point of time in the future:

> I'll be seeing you tomorrow *at exactly three o'clock in the afternoon*.
> At the theater tonight, the curtain will be rising *at eight*, so don't be late.

or to emphasize the duration of an event in the future:

> I'll be studying hard from now until the end of next week; it's finals time.
> They'll be staying at their place at the lake for the rest of the summer.

You will remember that we also use the simple future tense to express the occurrence or duration of an event in the future; the future continuous tense only adds emphasis:

> I will see (will be seeing) you soon.
> I will study (will be studying) hard from now until then.
> They will stay (will be staying) on their farm down in the South until the beginning of spring, and then they will come (will be coming) north to their place up in the mountains.

6. The simple future tense and its continuous form are not interchangeable in every case. Compare the differences in meaning:

> When you come home, we *will eat* dinner. (at that moment)
> When you come home, we *will be eating* dinner. (at that time)
> When you arrive at the reception, everyone *will be standing up*. (at that time)
> Everyone at the meeting will be sitting down, but when the President arrives, everyone *will stand up*. (at that moment)

77 yes-no questions in future tenses

1. In the simple future tense, *will* precedes the subject in yes–no questions:

> *Will you* be here on time? Yes, I will (shall).
> *Will they* probably arrive early? No, they won't.

2. *Will* also precedes the subject in the future continuous tense:

> *Will you* be turning off that radio soon?
> *Will she* be showing up soon?

3. When the verb *be* follows the subject, it may follow *will* in a yes–no answer, but its use is optional:

> Will *Margaret and Bob be* happy in their marriage? Yes, they *will* (*be*).
> Will *you be* studying this summer? No, I *won't* (*be*).

4. This optional use of *be* also occurs in some other patterns:

> You'll be turning on the TV soon, won't you (be)?
> I won't be seeing you soon, and neither will my sister (be).
> I'll be getting up early tomorrow, and my roommate will (be) too.

78 information questions in future tenses

1. In information questions in the simple future and the future continuous tenses, *will* precedes the subject:

> Where *will you* and your family eventually live?
> How long *will you* probably be working on your writing project?

2. The usual question form is not observed when an information word is the subject of a question:

> *What* will eventually happen to us?
> *Who* will probably be sitting in the class when you get there tomorrow?

3. Either a formal or informal style occurs in negative questions:

formal: Will you not be attending classes regularly?
informal: Won't you help me out?
formal: Why *will the government not* be lowering taxes?
informal: Why *won't the government* give us a tax break?

4. *Please* occurs with *won't you* in polite requests:

Won't you please fill this form out?
Won't you please stand over there?

Pronunciation note: *Won't you* frequently sounds like *won't-chew.*

79   regular and irregular past participles

The rules for spelling regular past participles are the same as those for spelling regular past forms (see 38). A list of past participles of commonly used irregular verbs will be found in Appendix 3 of *ESL Grammar Quiz Book.*

80   the present perfect tense; the duration of an event, *since* and *for*

1. To form the PRESENT PERFECT TENSE, we use the verb *have* as an auxiliary and a past participle as the main verb of a verb phrase. *Have* occurs as an -s form in the third person singular. *Not* is inserted between the auxiliary and the past participle in a negative verb phrase. *Haven't* is the contraction for *have not,* and *hasn't* is the contracted form of *has not.*

	singular			*plural*	
1st person	I	⎱		we	⎱
2nd person	you	⎰ have not (haven't) done		you	⎰ have not (haven't)
3rd person	he	⎱		they	
	she	⎰ has not (hasn't) done			
	it				

2. Contractions of *have* or *has* with subject pronouns occur in informal usage.

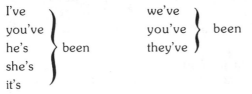

3. To determine whether the contraction 's is *has* or *is,* you can follow two general rules:

a. When a past participle (often preceded by an adverb) follows 's, it is the contraction of *has:*

It's (*has*) been nice to meet you.
He's (*has*) already done his chores.

b. When 's is followed by articles, adjectives, and *-ing* forms, it is the contraction of *is:*

It's (*is*) a cold night.
He's (*is*) careless.
She's (*is*) studying hard.

Note: Some past participles occur as adjectives:

It's (is) broken.   He's (is) retired.   She's (is) drunk.

4. The present perfect tense is used to express the duration of an event that began at a definite point in past time and has continued to the present and will probably continue into future time.

The United States *has been* an independent nation since July 4, 1776; it *has been* a republic for more than two hundred years.

5. When we express the duration of an event from past to present time and the amount of time is given, the preposition *for* is used in a prepositional phrase.

The earth has been in existence *for billions and billions of years.*
Buddhism has been a major religion *for more than two thousand years.*

The use of *for* is optional:

Hinduism has been the major religion of India (*for*) *more than four thousand years.*

6. A prepositional phrase with the preposition *since* is used when the exact moment, time, day, or year that the event began is stated:

The streets of the town have been quiet *since midnight.*
His mother and father have been married *since June 1, 1978.*
The Red Cross has been an international organization *since 1864.*

or when one event follows another:

He and his family have lived in a tent *since the flood.*
Some form of religion has been a strong force *since the early beginnings of man.*

7. Prepositional phrases with *since* or *for* usually occur in final position:

> The Eiffel Tower has stood in the middle of Paris *since 1889.*
> Islam has been the major religion in the Middle East *(for) more than 1500 years.*

They may also occur in initial position followed by a comma. In this case, *for* is not optional.

> *For more than sixty years,* the Soviet Union has been a communist state.
> *Since 1810,* the republic of Mexico has been independent from Spain.

> **Reminder:** *Since* is also used as a subordinate conjunction to introduce clauses of reason which answer questions with *why*:
>
> *Since he doesn't speak English,* it's difficult for him to find a job.

81 *since* in time clauses; *ago; ever*

1. *Since* occurs as a subordinate conjunction when it introduces a time clause (subordinate clause) to a complex sentence:

> He has been a new man *since he fell in love with his neighbor's daughter.*
> The people of that country have been in a state of terror *since their revolution began.*

> **Reminder:** A time phrase never has a subject or a verb, but a time clause always does. Compare:

time phrase	*time clause*
. . . since the beginning of the revolution	. . . since *the revolution began.*
. . . since the end of World War II.	. . . since *World War II ended.*

2. The adverb *ago* appears only with the simple past tense:

> He *moved* to this town two years *ago.*
> They *got* married five years *ago.*

However, *ago* may appear in a time clause or phrase introduced by *since* when the verb phrase in the main clause of a sentence is in the present perfect tense:

> He's *lived* with his aunt and uncle *since he moved to this town two years ago.*
> They've *lived* happily together *since their marriage five years ago.*

3. The adverb *ever,* in rather informal usage, may occur as an inten-sifier of the preposition *since* in a time phrase:

> We've been worried about our son *ever since* the beginning of the war.
> Their baby has been healthy *ever since* his birth.

It may also occur as an intensifier of the subordinate conjunction *since* in a time clause:

> We've been worried about our son *ever since* the war began.
> Their baby has been healthy *ever since* he was born.

As with time phrases, time clauses with *since* may occur in either initial or final position:

> Our neighbors have had their car *since 1940.*
> *Since they bought it in 1940,* our neighbors have had their car.

Much emphasis is added when a time clause occurs in initial position.

4. *Ever* also occurs in negative verb phrases; it follows *not:*

> I haven*'t ever* been in China.
> He's *not ever* voted in an election.

82 contrasting verb tenses

1. The simple present tense is not used for the duration of an event from past to present. Compare:

correct	*incorrect*
They have been married for five years.	They [are married] for five years.
We have lived here since 1980.	We [live] here since 1980.

Nor do we use the present continuous tense to express duration beginning in the past. Compare:

correct	*incorrect*
He has worked there for twenty years.	He [is working] there for twenty years.

The present perfect tense is not used to express an event at a definite time in the past. Compare:

correct	*incorrect*
I went there yesterday.	I [have gone] there yesterday.
He died five years ago.	He [has died] five years ago.

83 yes-no questions; *as long as*

1. *Have* or *has* precedes the subject in yes–no questions with the present perfect tense:

> *Have you* been a Christian all your life?
> *Has Zimbabwe* been an independent nation for a very long time?

2. In yes–no answers, *have* or *has* follows the subject of the answer:

> Has the patient felt well since her operation? Yes, *she has.* No, *she hasn't (has not).*
> Have you had this book for a long time? Yes, *I have.* No, *I haven't (have not).*

When the past participle *been* occurs as the main verb in a yes–no question, it may also occur in the short answer made in response; its use is optional:

> Have you *been* at this school since the beginning of the semester? Yes, I have (*been*). No, I haven't (*been*).
> Has Patricia *been* a happy person since her marriage a few years ago? Yes, she has (*been*). No, she hasn't (*been*).

3. The subordinate conjunction *as long as* means *during the time that* and is frequently used to introduce time clauses containing the present perfect tense:

> Terry has had his bicycle *as long as his father has had his car.*
> We have lived in our apartment *as long as you've lived in your house.*

We may abridge a clause introduced by *as long as:*

> Have you been a student *as long as she* (has)?
> He's had a car *as long as I* (have).

84 information questions

Have or *has* precedes the subject in information questions with the present perfect tense. (*For*) *how long,* or (*for*) *how many* + stated time, occurs in information questions asking the duration of an event from past to present time:

> (*For*) *how long have you* been a student at this school?
> (*For*) *how many months has your roommate* had his beard?

85 events at an indefinite time in the past; *recently, finally, just,* and *already*

1. Besides being used to express the duration of an event from a definite point in past time to the present, the present perfect tense is used to describe an event at an indefinite time in the past. Compare:

definite time in the past	*indefinite time in the past*
We rode on an elephant *yesterday.*	We have ridden on an elephant.
The sun rose at 6:30 *this morning.*	The sun has risen.

2. ADVERBS OF INDEFINITE TIME like *recently, finally, just,* and *already* regularly occur in verb phrases in the present perfect tense. Their usual position is following the auxiliary:

> We've *recently* seen birds flying north; spring *has finally* come.
> The cherry tree in our front yard *has just* blossomed.
> The days *have already* become longer; summer is coming.

3. *Just* occurs only within a verb phrase, but *recently, finally,* and *already* may appear in initial or final position as well as following the auxiliary. A comma is usually placed after an adverb occurring in initial position:

Recently, I've seen a ghost.	I've seen a ghost *recently.*
Finally, the bell has rung.	The bell has rung *finally.*
Already, his youth has passed.	His youth has passed *already.*

4. Adverbs of indefinite time often appear with the present perfect tense in compound verbs containing *one* auxiliary and two past participles:

> I've *recently seen and done* many fascinating things.
> Our team *has finally practiced hard and won* the championship.
> How good I feel! I've *just taken and passed* the final examination.

5a. When you hear a sentence like *She has recently fallen in love,* you might well respond, *How recent is recently?* The adverb can mean a week ago, a month ago, perhaps several months ago, or even a year ago. The period of time is very indefinite:

> Her life *has recently become* more exciting; she's found romance.
> *Recently,* he hasn't felt well, so he hasn't been working.

b. *Just* is more specific than *recently.* We do not know exactly when the event has taken place; however, we do know that it has happened close to the present time:

The home team *has just scored* a point, and the fans are cheering wildly.

Our baby boy *has just gotten* his first haircut, and he looks like a young man.

c. *Finally* conveys more than just a sense of time; the adverb suggests that we have been anticipating the event eagerly or anxiously:

The monsoon *has finally come* to an end; we're now waiting for the fall harvest.

He's *finally found* a job; he no longer needs to depend on his friends for money.

6. The idiom *at last,* which means *finally,* is often used with the present perfect tense; it may appear in final position:

She has found the man of her dreams *at last.*

or in initial position followed by a comma or an exclamation mark:

At last, their dreams have become a reality.

At last! I've finally gotten a perfect score on a quiz.

The expression may sometimes also be found within a verb phrase itself:

Our children *have at last come* home from their hike.

It's about time, another expression meaning *finally,* frequently accompanies sentences containing *finally* or *at last:*

It's about time! Winter has finally come to an end.

It's about time! My neighbor across the street has mowed his lawn at last.

The adverb *well* (meaning *it's about time*) is also a frequent companion to *finally* or *at last;* it may be followed by a comma or an exclamation mark:

Well, that student has at last asked a question that the professor cannot answer.

Well! Finally, my company has given me a promotion and raise in salary.

7. When the adverb *already* occurs in a verb phrase containing the present perfect tense, it usually suggests recent to fairly recent time in the past:

The mail carrier *has already come and gone.* (about an hour ago)

I've *already prepared* the dessert for tonight's dinner. (yesterday)

In some circumstances, however, *already* may appear in statements about the distant past:

> She's *already graduated* from the university. (seven years ago)
> He doesn't want to go to that country again; he's *already been* there. (ten years ago)

86 adverbs of indefinite time in yes-no questions; cause and effect

1. Adverbs of indefinite time usually follow the subject in yes–no questions:

> Have *you recently* had a medical checkup, Dr. Johnson?
> Has *he finally* proposed marriage to his girlfriend?
> Have *you just* come in out of the cold? Your hands are as cold as ice.
> Have *you already* finished breakfast and done the dishes?

2. Except for *just*, in less formal usage adverbs of indefinite time may occur in final position when a yes–no question is short:

> Have you seen a good boxing match *recently?*
> Has my secretary done something right *finally?*
> Have you taken and corrected the quiz *already?*

3. Although the present perfect tense is used to express events that occurred at an indefinite time in the past, they are directly related to events in present time because they are the cause (reason) for situations that now exist. We call this relationship the *cause and effect* (reason and situation) relationship. Compare:

cause (an event at an indefinite time in the past)	*effect (now)*
Our son *has finally come* home from his long and dangerous journey.	Everyone in the family *is* happy and relieved.
The curtain *has just risen.*	The play *is beginning* at last.
I've *already eaten* a lot.	I no longer *have* an appetite.

87 adverbs of indefinite time with the simple past tense

1. The adverbs of indefinite time also appear in verb phrases containing the simple past tense. If the adverb is *just, finally,* or *already,* adverbial expressions of definite time may follow at the end of the clause.

My next door neighbor *just got* a new lawnmower *last week*.
She *finally mowed* her lawn *yesterday morning*.
We *already went* shopping *yesterday*.

However, definite adverbs of time never occur with *recently*:

.   The post office *recently changed* my mailman's delivery route.
My neighbors on the corner *recently moved* to the Southwest.

2. In formal usage, *already* and *recently* do not ordinarily occur with the simple past tense. More formal usage requires that *already* and *recently* be used with phrases containing the present perfect tense or the simple present tense:

The sun *has already risen*, and a new day has begun.
She's studied English a long time; she *already knows* a lot about the language.
Madame Adikari *has recently changed* the color of her hair.

88   negative yes - no questions with adverbs of indefinite time

1. In informal usage, adverbs of indefinite time follow the subject in negative yes–no questions:

Haven't *you recently* had a serious operation?
Hasn't *this hurricane finally* come to an end?
Haven't *we already* had enough to eat, children?
Hasn't *your cousin just* inherited a million dollars?

Pronunciation note: *Haven't you* often sounds like *haven't-chew.*

2. In formal usage, the adverb follows *not:*

Has the Prime Minister *not recently* looked over this document?
Sir, have you *not just* put your foot in your mouth?
Have we *not already* discussed my problem enough, Professor?
Has the prisoner *not finally* realized his past mistakes?

3. Except for *just,* an adverb of time may also occur in final position:

Haven't you lost your wallet *recently*, Jim?
Hasn't the Judge made a decision *finally?*
Tommy, haven't you taken out the trash *already?*

Reminder: Negative questions are most frequently used to express surprise, seek confirmation, or show anger.

89 *any longer, anymore,* and *no longer*

1. The adverb *anymore* and the adverbial expression *any longer* are used in negatives and questions, usually in the final position of a clause or sentence:

> He and I have had several arguments; we seldom see each other *anymore.*
> Don't you go to the movies *anymore?* Have you grown tired of them?
> Mr. Hopper isn't working for this company *any longer;* in fact, he's gone into business on his own and is now our biggest competitor.

2. *No longer* usually precedes affirmative verb phrases:

> Our dog *no longer* has fleas; we've finally gotten rid of them with this flea powder.

The expression may follow the verb *be:*

> Our town (is) *no longer* is quiet and peaceful; it's become a big city.

90 *yet* in negative statements

1. The indefinite adverb of time *yet* shows expectation (something that we plan to do) and is always closely related to a coming event in future time:

> We haven't eaten dinner *yet.* (it's only five o'clock; we're eating at six)
> The class hasn't begun *yet.* (it's only 9:45; it begins at ten)

2. *Yet* usually occurs in the final position of a simple sentence, or in the final position of a main clause. The verb is in its negative form:

> You *haven't done anything* about the leaky faucet in the kitchen *yet.*
> The plane *hasn't taken off yet,* but all the passengers are strapped in their seats and ready to go.

3. In more formal usage, and sometimes informal, *yet* may follow *not:*

> We have *not yet* entered the third millennium. **or** We haven't *yet* entered the third millennium.
> They have *not yet* decided on a name for their new baby. **or** They haven't *yet* decided on a name for their new baby.

4. When a negative word occurs in a subject, an affirmative verb phrase follows:

> No one *has gone* beyond the moon *yet.* Not one of you *has learned* enough *yet.*

In such sentences *yet* may occur within a verb phrase:

> No one *has yet seen* these plans. Not one of us *has yet made* our fortune.

91 *still* in the simple present tense

1. The adverb *still* usually has the meaning of *continuance:*

> Everyone in the family is worried; their father is still sick. (He has been sick, and he hasn't gotten well yet.)

It can also have the meaning of *nevertheless:*

> He has a good education, but he still doesn't have a good job. (Despite the fact that he has a good education, he doesn't have a good job.)

2. *Still* usually precedes verb phrases:

> Our son *still sings* soprano in the church choir; his voice hasn't changed yet.
> That student *still doesn't speak* English fluently; she hasn't mastered the language yet.

3. *Still* most often follows the verb *be:*

> I *am still* tired; I haven't slept enough yet.
> They *are still* happy together; they haven't fallen out of love yet.

For greater emphasis, *still* may precede the verb *be:*

> I know you disagree with your mother and father, but they *still are* your parents, and you should love, respect, and obey them as much as you can.
> He's gone to his lawyer about the problem, but he *still is* in trouble with the Internal Revenue Service.

4. In negative verb phrases, *still* almost always precedes the verb *be:*

> I'm happy with our new house, but my wife *still isn't* accustomed to it.
> Everyone is waiting for the guests of honor, but they *still aren't* here.

But for greater emphasis, and in more formal usage, the adverb may follow the verb:

> She is dressed and ready to go out, but her husband *is still* not out of his bathrobe.
> They speak English well, but they *are still* not ready to enter the university.

5. *Still* frequently appears with negative verb phrases containing *ever*:

> He loves the movies, but he *still doesn't ever go.*
> I don't work at night, but I'm *still not ever* home during the evening.

92   *still* in the present continuous tense

1. The adverb *still* may take a variety of positions in relation to the auxiliary *be* in a verb phrase containing the present continuous tense:

> I'm *still* not feeling well even though I've taken my medicine.
> I *still am* not making social appointments; I'm too busy with my projects at work.
> They're not happy here, but they're *still* living here.
> They *still are* moving away even though they want to stay.

2. To emphasize the habituality of an event, the adverb *always* follows *still*:

> He has everything he needs, but he is *still always* complaining.
> His dentist says he has no cavities, but his teeth are *still always* aching.
> Her feet don't really bother her, but she *still* is *always* complaining.

93   yes-no questions with *still*

In both the simple present tense and the present continuous tense, the adverb *still* follows the subject in yes–no questions:

> Does *your nephew still* go to school? Yes, he hasn't graduated yet.
> Do *you still* smoke? No, I have finally given up the dirty habit.
> Does *your niece still* usually walk to school? Yes, she hasn't gotten a bike yet.
> Are *you still* always worrying about your son? No, he has finally grown out of his adolescent ways.
> Are *your mosquito bites still* bothering you? No, I've just put some ointment on them.

94   yes-no questions with *yet*

1. Yet occurs in yes–no questions in the present perfect tense more frequently than the other adverbs of indefinite time. *Yet* usually appears at the end of a question:

> Have Marcia and her boyfriend made up their minds *yet?*
> Have the counterrevolutionaries attacked the rebels' strongholds *yet?*

In more formal usage, *yet* may follow the subject:

Has *the Brazilian Ambassador yet* called on the Pope?

2. Yes–no questions with *yet* are usually negative; we may observe either a formal or informal style:

informal: Haven't you finished your breakfast *yet?*
formal: Have you not finished your breakfast *yet?* **or** *Have you not yet* finished your breakfast?
informal: Son, *haven't you* cut your beard off yet?
formal: Son, *have you not* cut your beard off yet? **or** Son, *have you not yet* cut your beard off?

Note: *Yet* may appear with the simple present tense:

They *don't have* any children *yet.* (*meaning* They *haven't had* any children yet.)
He's only sixteen years old; he *isn't* a man *yet.* (*meaning* He *hasn't become* a man yet.)

However, *yet* occurs most frequently with the present perfect tense, even though in less formal usage the adverb sometimes occurs with the simple past tense:

sometimes: Did you *do* the job *yet?* No, I *didn't do* it yet.
more common: Have you *done* the job *yet?* No, I *haven't done* it yet.

95   information questions with *yet*

As in all negative information questions, *why* is the usual information word in negative questions with *yet*:

informal: Why *haven't you* dished out the food yet?
formal: Why *have you not* dished out the food yet? **or** Why *have you not yet* dished out the food?
informal: Why *haven't we* found peace yet?
formal: Why *have we not* found peace yet? **or** Why *have we not yet* found peace?

Pronunciation reminder: *Haven't you* frequently sounds like *haven't-chew.*

96   *yet* with abridged clauses and infinitives

1. Clauses of contrast containing abridged clauses and infinitives frequently accompany main clauses with the present perfect tense and *yet:*

He *hasn't ever run out of* money *yet*, but he *expects to* soon.
I *haven't gone* out with a movie star *yet*, but perhaps someday I *will*.

2. Most often, an abridged clause following *yet* contains *will* or *be going to:*

We haven't reached the summit yet, but *we will* (reach it with a little bit of luck and a lot of determination).
I haven't gone to Africa yet, but *I'm going to* (go on a safari there this coming summer).

3. Abridged infinitives may occur after the verbs *hope, want, expect,* and the phrase *would like:*

We haven't made a great fortune yet, but we *hope to* (make one).
We haven't yet gone to Kathmandu, but we *want to* (go on a trip there).
He hasn't won any money in the lottery yet, but he *expects to* (win a lot).
I haven't yet ridden on a roller coaster, but I'*d like to* (ride on one).

Often, it is necessary to put a pronoun object between the verb and *to:*

He hasn't quit his job yet, but his wife *wants him to* (quit it).
No, the bell hasn't rung yet, but I *expect it to* (ring shortly).
Madame Grimaldi, we have not yet heard you sing an Italian folk song, and *we'd like you to* (sing one for us).

Note: Pronoun objects do not occur with the verb *hope*.

4. The adverbial expression *any minute* (hour, day, etc.) *now* may follow abridged infinitives and clauses:

The monsoon hasn't arrived yet, but we expect it to *any day now*. (It's already arrived in Bombay, so it'll be here in Delhi soon.)
The movie hasn't begun yet, but it will *any second now*. (The lights have already lowered, and the curtain is opening.)

The *now* in the expression may be omitted:

My parents haven't yet called me up this month, but I expect them to *any day* (now).

5. The verbal phrase *be about to* is occasionally seen and heard as an abridged infinitive:

I haven't lost my temper yet, but I'*m about to*.
I haven't sneezed yet, but I'*m just about to*.

97 *have yet* + an infinitive

1. In rather formal usage, the verbal phrase *have* (has) *yet* + an infinitive sometimes occurs:

> The Minister of Defense has thought over the dilemma for some time; however, he *has yet to draw* any conclusions. (*meaning* he hasn't drawn any conclusions yet)
> The government has already made up its mind, but it *has yet to make* the announcement of its decision. (*meaning* it hasn't made its announcement yet)

2. For added emphasis, *still* may precede *have* (has) *yet:*

> I've worked for that company for three months, but they *still have yet to pay* me a dime.
> Grandpa has lived a long and rich life, but he feels he *still has yet to see and do* a great many things.

98 *still* with the present perfect tense

1. The adverb *still* does not ordinarily appear in affirmative statements with the present perfect tense; it is often found, however, preceding negative verb phrases:

> The world *still has not found* peace. (*meaning* it hasn't found peace yet)
> Our new hen *still hasn't laid an egg.* (*meaning* she hasn't laid an egg yet)

In more formal usage it may also sometimes follow the auxiliary:

> We *have still* not visited the Vatican even though it is the most important place to see in Rome.
> They *have still* not done any favors for me even though I've done many for them.

2. *Ever* makes a frequent appearance with *still* in the present perfect tense; it always follows *not:*

> Though she's lived in New York for many years, she still hasn't *ever* seen the view of the city from the top of the Empire State Building.
> Although I know Picasso was one of the greatest artists of his time, I still have *not ever* enjoyed his paintings except for those painted during his Blue Period.

3. In less formal usage, *yet* may appear at the end of a clause or a statement with *still:*

> No. 66 still hasn't scored a point *yet* even though he's playing far better than anyone else on the team.
> We've recently bought a new cow, but she still hasn't produced much milk *yet.*

4. Verb phrases with *still* are more emphatic than those with *yet. Still* may convey the feeling of great disappointment:

> They *still* haven't found their Shangri-la (enchanted place); they've been traveling around the world for years looking for it.

Still might very well also be used to show anger or irritation:

> Darn it! I *still* haven't gotten rid of these darn mosquitoes.
> Tiffany, it's almost midnight, and you *still* haven't gone to bed yet.

We also often use it to express surprise:

> It's very bright out, but the sun *still* hasn't risen.
> Their daughter is almost thirteen years old, and she *still* hasn't lost her baby teeth.

5. *Still* sometimes occurs in initial position; it is followed by a comma in writing and a pause in speech:

> *Still,* (pause) the man she admires in the office hasn't asked her out yet.

or it may appear in final position preceded by a comma:

> Ladies and Gentlemen, we haven't gotten rid of corruption in our society, (pause) *still.*

6. *What* as an exclamatory word frequently occurs with *still:*

> *What!* The police still haven't found the lost child?
> *What!* The plumber still hasn't fixed the leak in your bathroom?

> **Note:** The adjective *still* is often heard in the idiom *hold still* (remain still):
>
> I'd like to take a picture of the baby, but she won't *hold still.*
> *Hold still,* Jamie, the doctor wants to give you a shot; it won't hurt.

99 *still* in negative questions

1. *Still* follows the subject in yes–no questions with the present perfect tense:

> You mean your gas and electric bill isn't correct—have *you still* paid it?
> You say you don't like that doctor—have *you still* gone to him again?

2. *Still* in present perfect affirmative questions is not common; the adverb most often occurs in negative yes–no and information questions. *Still* always precedes *not* in such questions.

> Andy, have you *still not* washed the dishes from dinner? It's almost time for bed.
> Sir, have you *still not* listened to the workers' demands for better working conditions? Why have they *still not* struck for higher pay?

100   repeated events in the past

1. Another frequent use of the present perfect tense is to express events that have taken place once or more than once in past time:

> The United States *has had* many fine presidents and quite a few poor ones.
> Clara, if I *have told* you once, I *have told* you three times not to tease the cat.

2. Expletive *there* frequently occurs when we use the present perfect tense for repeated events in the past:

> *There have been* two major events in my life this past year: my marriage and the birth of my son.
> *There have been* quite a few volcanic eruptions and earthquakes in the western part of the country in recent years.

3. When the present perfect tense is used for repeated events in past time, there usually is the expectation that the event may occur again in future time:

> The strange old woman said to me, "If people who say a cat has nine lives are correct, my cat, Fluffy, will have two more—she *has already lived* seven."
> There *have been* many wars, revolutions, and crises of one nature or the other since the end of the Second World War, and there will quite likely be a great many more before we enter the new millennium.

4. When we express repeated events in past time with the simple past tense, there is no expectation that the event will be repeated. Compare:

the simple past tense	*the present perfect tense*
Many things happened yesterday. (yesterday is over)	Many things have happened today. (today hasn't come to an end yet)
John's grandfather saw and did many things. (he isn't living now)	John has seen and done many things. (he expects to see and do a great many more)

101 questions about repeated events in the past

1. When we ask information questions with the present perfect tense about repeated events in past time, the phrase *how many times* is often employed, sometimes preceded by *approximately,* or *about* in less formal usage:

> *How many times* have you gone to the barber since the beginning of the year?
> Professor, *approximately how many times* has the earth revolved around the sun?
> *About how many times* has Jackie Jacobs hit a home run this season?

How many + a plural noun is also frequently employed:

> *How many landings* has man made on the moon?
> Approximately *how many classes* have you been absent from this semester?

2. Expletive *there* is inserted between the auxiliary and the past participle of a verb phrase in yes–no and information questions:

> *Have there been* any major earthquakes in the world this year?
> How many forest fires *have there been* in the Northwest this fall?

3. The adverb *only* is often used to emphasize the number of times an event has occurred:

> He's almost fifty now, and he's had *only one* important romance in his life.
> She's met him *only once,* but she'll always remember his beautiful smile.
> They've gone to Paris *only twice,* and they're dying to go there again.
> He's tried practicing yoga *only three times,* and he's eager to try it again.

4. *Only* is commonly used in short responses to information questions:

> How many bales of hay has the elephant eaten this week? . . . *only two.*
> How many times has he gone out with his fiancée? . . . *only three.*
> How many times have you gone around the world? . . . *only once.*

> **Note:** *Thrice* (meaning *three times*) is very old-fashioned; it rarely occurs these days.

5. Complete sentences containing negative verb phrases with *never* or *ever* often occur in response to information questions about repeated events in the past:

How many times have you been in love? *I've never been in love.*
How many times have you drunk champagne? *I've never drunk it.*
How many times has she taken you out? *She hasn't ever taken me out.*

102 negative verb phrases with *ever*

1. *Ever* most often occurs in negative verb phrases with the present perfect tense:

Life has *not ever* been better than it is now.
The people in the south of the country haven*'t ever* gotten along with the people in the north.

However, when the subject of a clause or sentence is a negative word or a word that has a negative connotation, *ever* follows the auxiliary of a verb phrase:

No one in the world *has ever* been so nice to me as you have.
Only two of my good friends *have ever* had a successful marriage.

2. *Yet* may appear at the beginning of a main clause; when it does, it has the meaning of *however*:

He's worked hard all his life, *yet* (however) he has no money in the bank.

103 questions with *ever*

1. *Ever* follows the subject in yes–no and information questions:

Have *you ever* seen a ghost?
Has *your boss ever* done any of your work?
What have *I ever* done to make you so angry?

2. In negative questions, we may observe either a formal or informal style; *ever* follows *not* in formal usage:

"Have you *not ever* trusted me?" his lawyer asked.
"Why have we *not ever* had a serious argument?" he asked his wife.

In informal usage, *ever* follows the subject:

Haven't *you ever* been in some kind of danger?
Why hasn't *he ever* fixed breakfast for his wife?

104 the present perfect continuous tense; lately

1. To form the PRESENT PERFECT CONTINUOUS TENSE, we use *have* and *been* (as a second auxiliary) and a present participle as a main verb. *Have* occurs as an *-s* form in the third person singular. *Not* is inserted between *have* and *been* in negative verb phrases.

	singular		**plural**	
1st person	I		we	
2nd person	you	have (not) been doing	you	have (not) been doing
3rd person	he		they	
	she	has (not) been doing		
	it			

2. In yes–no and information questions, a subject follows *have (has)*:

> *Has the world* been making progress toward a lasting peace?
> How long *have you* been living here?

3. The form is used to emphasize the duration of an event that began at a definite point of time in the past and has continued to the present and possibly into the future:

> *We've been living* in Paradise ever since we bought our new house.
> He's *been smoking* a long time—since he was sixteen to be exact.

4. For expressing the duration of an event, the present perfect tense and its continuous form are essentially interchangeable; the continuous form only emphasizes the duration:

> They've *been living* (or *have lived*) in a tree house for five years.
> Our little boy *hasn't been wearing* (or *hasn't worn*) diapers for more than six months.

5. For expressing an event of a temporary nature, the present perfect continuous tense and the present continuous tense are interchangeable:

> I've *been using* (or *am using*) my neighbor's lawnmower for the time being.
> He's *been walking* (or *is walking*) to work temporarily.

6. The present perfect continuous tense is also used for expressing repeated events in the past; however, we do not use *times* with the form:

> The workers *have been making* demands. (*but* The workers *have made* demands three times.)

Nor do we use *once* or *twice*:

> I've *been going* to the beach a lot. (*but* I've *gone* to the beach once or twice this summer.)

7. *Just* and *recently* may occur with the form; they follow the first auxiliary:

Well, hello; I've *just* been thinking about you.
Yes, she *has recently* been making a great many new friends.

Always sometimes occurs; it also follows the first auxiliary:

Ever since we moved into this apartment, our landlord *has always* been complaining.

Never, already, finally, and *how many times* never occur with the present perfect continuous tense.

8. As in the present continuous tense, nonaction verbs such as *be, cost, need,* and *love* do not ordinarily occur in the present perfect continuous tense; however, when we express a temporary feeling or action, a nonaction verb occurs as a main verb in a phrase:

I've been *loving* these moments with you. (*but* I *love* you.)
I've been *wanting* to tell you about something for a long time—may I tell you now? (*but* I *want* peace and happiness.)

Remember when adjectives follow the verb *be,* the verb is sometimes used as a present participle (main verb).

You've been *being difficult,* young man; now eat up your spinach.
I've been *being foolish* in this matter, haven't I?

9. The nonaction verb *have* meaning to show possession does not occur in the present perfect continuous tense; only the present perfect tense is used:

He *has had* his bicycle ever since he was a boy.
We *have had* our farm in the country for thirty years.

However, the verb *have* occurs idiomatically with certain nouns in the present perfect continuous tense:

The mechanic has been having *difficulty* fixing our car.
Our club has recently been having a lot of *parties, dances, barbecues* (cookouts), *contests,* and even *lotteries.*
I've been having a lot of tennis *lessons* this summer.
I've been having nothing but *problems* and *dilemmas* all day long.
Fortunately, we haven't been having much *rain* or *snow* this winter.
Nor have we been having many *storms* or *blizzards.*
What a wonderful (terrible) *time* we've been having on our vacation!
What kind of *trouble* have you been having at the factory?

10. The adverb *lately* means *recently;* it most often occurs in final position.

We've been doing a lot of new and exciting things *lately.*
Many new ideas have been running through my mind *lately.*

It may appear, however, in initial position followed by a comma:

> *Lately,* a lot of funny things have been happening in my life.
> *Lately,* your son has been making much more progress in the class.

105   *so far, until now,* and *now*

1. The expressions *so far* and *until now* commonly occur in sentences containing the present perfect tense or its continuous form. They usually appear in final position, but they also make a frequent appearance in initial position followed by a comma:

> We've been having wonderful weather on this vacation *so far.*
> *So far,* we haven't had any cold, fog, or rain; we've been lucky.
> The patient has been feeling well *until now.*
> *Until now,* he hasn't had a fever, chills, or loss of appetite.

2. *So far* means *up to the moment;* the expression conveys the meaning that an event that has been taking place for some time will continue into future time:

> We've had good weather this year *so far.* (we still have good weather)
> It's been raining for a week *so far.* (it's still raining)

The expression is also used with repeated events in the past:

> They've lived in ten different houses *so far.* (and they expect to move again soon)
> Our star player has scored thirty-seven points *so far.* (and he's going to score a great many more)

3. *Until now* also means *up to the moment;* however, the expression conveys the meaning that an event is no longer taking place:

> We've been having a lot of rain *until now.* (it stopped raining this morning)
> *Until now,* I have had everything I needed. (I need a car now for my new job)

4. *Until* often combines with *today, tonight,* etc.

> Look at that rain! We've been having perfect weather *until today.*
> She hasn't been feeling well *until this evening.* (The medicine she took this morning has certainly helped her out.)
> I've always liked my boss *until this morning.* (Why did he give my desk to that newcomer?)

5. When *now* is used with the present perfect tense or its continuous form, it is similar in meaning to *so far:*

> It's been snowing for five days *now* (so far).
> My wife and I have lived in this town for ten years *now* (so far).

106   questions

> **Note:** When the past participle *been* occurs as an auxiliary in the verb phrase of a yes–no question, it may also occur in the short answer made in response; its use is optional:
>
> Have Patricia and David *been* speaking to each other since their recent divorce?
> Yes, they have (*been*).   No, they haven't (*been*).

107   the present perfect tense in subordinate clauses

1. The present perfect tense often occurs in adverbial subordinate clauses introduced by *although* (*though, even though*) and *because* (*since*).

> Although he *hasn't caught on to* the joke, he's still laughing.
> He doesn't speak English well because he *hasn't ever studied* it at a school.

2. With subordinate adverbial time clauses introduced by *until* and *as soon as,* the present perfect tense and the simple present tense are essentially interchangeable for expressing events taking place in future time:

> I'm not going to tell you my joke *until you've told* (or *tell*) me yours.
> The rate of inflation will go up *as soon as the price of oil has risen* (or *rises*) *again.*

In such sentences, the present perfect tense emphasizes that the event in the subordinate clause will be completed *before* the event expressed in the main clause.

108   the present perfect tense with *when, before,* and *after*

As with *until* and *as soon as,* in time clauses introduced by *when, before,* and *after,* the present perfect tense and the simple present tense are more or less interchangeable for expressing events occurring in future time; it's mainly a question of emphasis:

We'll have a big celebration *when you have graduated* (or *graduate*) *next June.*

Mom is going to make a cake *before we've gotten* (or *get*) *home from school.*

My father won't be working anymore *after he has passed* (or *passes*) *the age of 65.*

109 *have got*

1. Idiomatically, we use the verb phrase *have* (*has*) *got* to show possession in the same way that we use the verb *have:*

> I *have got* (or *have*) a secret; my roommate *has got* (or *has*) one, too.

Note: The past participle *gotten* never occurs in this form.

2. For showing possession, *have got* does not ordinarily occur in formal writing—it is very informal. Because of its informality, *have* (*has*) and subject pronouns most often occur in a contracted form:

> *I've* got it, *you've* got it, *she's* got it, *they've* got it; *we've* all got the answer.

3. Negative verb phrases are frequently heard:

> I *haven't got* time to horse around today; I *haven't got* a minute to waste.
>
> He's in a difficult financial situation; he *hasn't got* a dime to his name.

4. Yes–no and information questions sometimes occur in American English:

> Excuse me, what time *have you got? Have you got* a watch on?

However, asking questions with *have got* occurs more frequently in British usage. A speaker in the United States is more likely to say:

> Excuse me, what time *do you have? Do you have* a watch on?

5. We cannot show possession with *have got* in past time, but we can for the future:

> I've got a date for *next Saturday night,* and so has my brother.

Pronunciation note: The indefinite article *a* often follows *have got;* when we are speaking rapidly, *got a* frequently sounds like *gotta:*

> Ronnie loves cars; he's *"gotta"* beautiful 1950 Buick convertible in perfect condition.

110 *have got to* + a base form

1. *Have got to* + a base form is used to express a strong sense of necessity; it has the same meaning as the modal auxiliary *must:*

> I've *got to* (must) get some gas for the car; we've almost run out.
> She's *got to* (must) change her schedule at work; it's killing her.

Note: The past participle *gotten* never appears in this form.

2. The adverb *just,* serving as an intensifier, is often inserted between *have* and *got to:*

> I've *just got to* lie down; I'm completely worn out.
> Andy Atkins *has just got to* settle down; he's still living like a nomad, and he's almost 45 years old.

3. Like the modal *must,* the idiom *have got to* may also express strong recommendation:

> You've *got to* marry me, Darling; I'm the person for you.
> You've *just got to* read this book; it's fascinating.

4. Yes–no and information questions with *have got to* sometimes occur:

> *Has your son* got to go back to school? No, he hasn't.
> *Have you* got to get up early tomorrow morning? Yes, I have.
> What time *have you* got to get up every day? . . . too early.

In American English, however, speakers are more accustomed to using the idiom *have to* in their questions, which also expresses necessity but to a lesser degree:

> Does your son *have to* go back to school? No, he doesn't.
> Do you *have to* get up early tomorrow morning? Yes, I do.
> What time do you *have to* get up every day? . . . earlier than I'd like to.

5. Negative verb phrases with *have got to* (e.g. *haven't got to*) rarely occur in either American or British usage. Both American and British speakers use *don't* (*doesn't*) *have to* for expressing lack of necessity:

> I *don't have to* get up early tomorrow.
> She *doesn't have to* go to the dentist.

Note: If the negative of *have got to* is used, it is formed with only *not*—never *do not*. Compare:

correct	*incorrect*
I *haven't* got to get up early tomorrow.	I [don't] got to get up early tomorrow.

Pronunciation note: When one is speaking very quickly, *got to* may sound like *gotta:*

You've *"gotta"* get busy, Mr. Brown, or else you'll lose your position.

Reminder: *Have got to* expresses necessity, but *have got* shows possession:

You've *got* (have) a beautiful smile, Miss.
You've *got to* (must) smile at all the customers, Jason, even though you don't like some of them.

111 questions with *how come*

1. *How come* means *why.* It precedes the subject in questions, and the verb phrases that follow are most often in their negative form. Questions with *how come* suggest mild surprise or irritation.

How come you haven't gone jogging today, Mr. Atlas?
How come you didn't want to go out with me last Saturday night?

2. Even though *how come* means *why,* note that the subject precedes the verb in a question:

How come she hasn't got a dictionary today?
How come I put an X in that blank?

In questions with *why,* the subject always follows the auxiliary:

Why *haven't you* got a dictionary today?
Why *did I* put an X in that blank?

112 *even* in negative verb phrases

For added emphasis, we may use the adverb *even* in negative verb phrases; it always follows *not:*

They're extremely poor; they *haven't even* got a roof over their heads.
Baby Bobby doesn't have his pants on; he *doesn't even* have his shirt on.
He'll never give anything away; he *won't even* give away old newspapers.
When I gave him his birthday present, he didn't say anything; he *didn't even* say thank you.

113 *another* versus *other(s)*

1. The pronoun *another* occurs only with singular nouns:

> I must buy *another dictionary;* the one I have is hopelessly out of date.
> Two children sleep in this room; *another child* sleeps in the room above this one.

Another may appear alone or be accompanied by *one* as a pronoun substitute:

> My dictionary is out of date; I should buy *another* (*one*).
> Would you like another cup of tea? Yes, thank you, I'd enjoy *another* (*one*).

2. *Other* usually occurs with plural nouns:

> There are *other people* in this family besides you, Mark; try not to be so thoughtless.
> There are *other plates* in that cupboard; would you please get three.

However, when *other* is preceded by *the, this, some, any,* or *each,* it may appear with a singular noun:

> Yes, this room is large, but *the other room* is even larger.
> I don't want my apartment to be painted red, yellow, or blue; *any other color* will do.

It may also appear alone or precede *one:*

> This stone is a real diamond; the *other* (*one*) is a fake, but it's hard to tell the difference, isn't it?

3. *Others* refers to only plural nouns, but it always occurs alone; it never precedes a noun:

> These students will take the examination today; the *others* will take it tomorrow.
> I'll give these out; would you please pass out the *others.*

4. Both *another* and *other* may have the meaning of *different:*

> Besides this one, is there *another* (different) *road* to Mexico City?
> Yes, there are *other* (different) *roads,* but they're far worse than the one we're on—the others are jammed with traffic all the time.

114 the past perfect tense

1. The PAST PERFECT TENSE is used to express an event that occurred before another in past time:

When my alarm clock rang, I *had woken* up. (before it rang)
When I entered the room, the class *had begun.* (before I entered the room)

2. To form the past perfect tense, *had,* the past form of *have,* is employed as an auxiliary in all persons, and a past participle is the main verb in a verb phrase:

	singular		*plural*	
1st person	I		we	
2nd person	you	had done	you	had done
3rd person	he		they	
	she			
	it			

Note: The past perfect tense is also called the PLUPERFECT TENSE.

3. In less formal usage, contractions of *had* and subject pronouns occur:

By the time (when) the meeting ended, *I'd* gone to sleep.
Prior to (before) his accident, *he'd* been as healthy as any man.

I			we		
you		'd done	you		'd done
he			they		
she					

Pronunciation note: There is no written contracted form for *it had;* however, in speaking, *it had* often sounds like *it-hid.*

4. For determining whether the contraction *'d* is *had* or *would,* two general rules to remember are:

a. When a past participle (often preceded by an adverb) or the word *better* follows *'d,* it is the contraction of *had:*

I'd (had) *just arrived* when you left.
You'd (had) *better* be on time.

b. When *'d* is followed by a base form or the word *rather,* it is the contraction of *would:*

I'd (would) *like* a cola, please.
I'd (would) *rather* have love than money.

5. In negative verb phrases, *not* follows the auxiliary:

Prior to the French Revolution, the aristocrats *had not* understood the needs of the common people.

The pianist *had not* had enough practice prior to the concert; consequently, she didn't play as well as she could have.

Hadn't, the contraction of *had not,* is seen and heard in less formal usage:

He ended up in prison even though he *hadn't* done anything wrong.

Although the terrorists *hadn't* given up, they were negotiating with the government officials.

6. Since the past perfect tense is most often used for an event preceding another single event in past time, the form nearly always occurs in a complex sentence containing a main and subordinate clause. In such sentences, the simple past tense may be used in the subordinate clause, and the past perfect tense is employed in the main clause. The event in the main clause preceded the event in the subordinate clause. Compare:

subordinate clause	*main clause*
When he *graduated* from college,	he *had been* a student for sixteen years. (before he finally graduated)
When she *sat down* to dinner,	she *hadn't eaten* all day. (before she finally sat down)

7. The past perfect tense may also be used in a subordinate clause; the simple past tense appears in the main clause. In this case, the event in the subordinate clause preceded the event in the main clause:

When the author *had finished* his second book, he immediately *started* on his third.

Because *he'd fought* for his ideals, the revolutionary *was hanged.*

Although the Indian tribes *had fought* bravely to protect their lands, the Union armies *crushed* them with their more advanced warfare and weaponry.

8. We occasionally use the past perfect tense in subordinate clauses introduced by *after* or *before:*

After she *had thought* about the situation for a week, it was still difficult for her to make a thoughtful decision.

Before she'd *made up* her mind, she'd *done* a lot of thinking.

In modern usage, speakers and writers tend to replace the form with the simple past tense:

After I *studied* (*had studied*), I listened to some music on the radio for a while and played with my cat.

Before she *got* (*had gotten*) married, her life was more interesting and exciting.

115 adverbs with the past perfect tense

As with the present perfect tense, the adverbs *already, finally, just,* and *recently* make frequent appearances in verb phrases containing the past perfect tense; they immediately follow the auxiliary:

> I'*d already* studied English quite a bit when I started this course.
> When my friend and I arrived in Kyoto, the cherry blossoms *had just* come out, and many women were wearing kimonos.
> When I first met Paula Bowers in Honolulu, she'*d recently* moved there from Pago Pago, where she'd been a reporter for a local newspaper.

Just and *recently* are sometimes combined:

> When he went back to Illinois for a family visit last summer, a tornado had *just recently* come through his hometown and completely destroyed his parents' house; they were staying at a hotel for the time being, so he had to stay at the YMCA.

116 *never, before,* and *ever*

1a. In a sentence in a past tense, the adverb *never* is nearly always accompanied by *before;* it most frequently appears at the end of a main clause:

> Until I went riding yesterday, I'd *never* ridden on a horse *before*.
> Until we went to India, we'd *never* seen a snake charmer *before*.

b. For emphasis, but in more formal usage, *before* sometimes follows *never* directly:

> When he went north to live, study, and work, he'd *never before* seen snow, nor had he *ever* been in such a cold climate.
> When Juliet fell in love with Romeo, she had *never before* been so happy.

c. *Before* may also occur at the beginning of a subordinate clause:

> *Before* he was twenty, he'd never shaved once.
> Their grandmother had never flown *before* she went on her trip to Brazil last year; it was an exciting event for her.

d. For emphasis, and in less formal usage, *before* is occasionally found in the same sentence at the beginning of a subordinate clause as well as in the final position in a main clause:

Before they went to China, they'd never eaten dog *before*.
Before Señora Lopez met Mrs. Bridges, she'd never met a North
American woman *before*.

2. The adverb *ever* usually occurs in negative verb phrases:

Romeo *hadn't ever been* really happy until he met Juliet, the woman of
his dreams.
In Japan when we spent the night at a small country inn, we *hadn't
ever slept* so low on the floor before.

When the subject of a clause or a sentence is a negative word or a word of
negative connotation, *not* is deleted in order to avoid a double negative:

Until they went to Thailand, *only* her husband *had ever* been there
before.
Until I took all my friends to the zoo for a picnic, *none* of them *had ever*
been there before.

117   *still* in the simple past tense; *anyhow* and *anyway*

1. In the simple past tense and its continuous form, *still* follows the
verb *be* on most occasions:

Although he was nearly forty years old, he *was still* the world's top tennis player.
He *was still acting* as the president of the company even though he'd
made a great many foolish and expensive mistakes.

For emphasis, however, *still* is sometimes put before the verb *be*:

She *still was picking* on him all the time even though he'd begged her
to stop.

2. *Still* usually precedes negative verb phrases with the verb *be*:

Though he'd carefully followed his friend's directions, he *still wasn't
doing* the exercise correctly.

But on some occasions, for emphasis, *still* may follow the verb *be* in
negative verb phrases:

Although he *was still* not ready to challenge the world champion, his
manager forced him to do it.

3. With all other verbs in the simple past tense, *still* nearly always
precedes a verb phrase:

Though the pitcher hadn't thrown the ball very fast, the catcher *still
didn't catch it.*

My neighbors *still cut down* their beautiful cherry tree although it hadn't died. They said it had been blocking out the sun.

4. The adverb *anyhow,* and *anyway* in less formal usage, frequently occurs in clauses of unexpected result introduced by *but:*

Our team played as hard as they ever had, but we lost the game *anyhow (anyway)*.
She was quite tired, but she went out dancing *anyway (anyhow)*.

Anyhow (anyway) may also occur in a main clause of unexpected result combined with a subordinate clause of concession:

Even though he knew it was strictly against the law, he parked his car in front of the fire hydrant *anyhow*.
Yes, he was holding a job *anyway* even though he didn't have the proper working papers.

5. Although the pattern is redundant, and it is not considered good usage, in informal usage *still* and *anyhow (anyway)* may appear together in the same clause:

He hates to do it, but he *still* jogs five miles a day *anyway*.

118   *still* **with the past perfect tense**

1. In the past perfect tense, *still* rarely occurs in affirmative verb phrases; it almost always precedes *had not:*

When the enemy conquered the country, they *still had not* conquered the people.
When I last spoke to my parents out in Samoa on the phone, they *still hadn't* gotten rid of the termites in the foundation of our house.

2. Besides being used for expressing an event before an event in past time, we often use the past perfect tense to express the duration of an event that preceded another in past time:

When they moved out of their house some years ago, they had lived in it *since 1933*.
When they finally sold their antique car (a beautiful 1927 Cadillac sedan), they had had it *for seventeen years*.

3. The past perfect tense also has a third major use: to express repeated events before another single event in past time:

Dickie had already had *three* pieces of chicken when he had another one.

The enemy forces had already made *two* major attacks since early that morning when they suddenly attacked once again with even greater force.

When the bell rang, *twelve* students had already arrived, and three more were expected.

119   the past perfect continuous tense

1. The PAST PERFECT CONTINUOUS TENSE is used to emphasize the duration of an event preceding another in past time. It is essentially interchangeable with the past perfect tense:

> When the rose bushes had finally been planted, I *had been working* (*had worked*) in the garden all day long.

However, with action words like *live, do, work,* and *smoke,* speakers and writers tend to prefer emphasizing the continuing nature of the event by using the past perfect continuous tense rather than the past perfect:

> They'd *been living* together for three years when they suddenly broke up.
> I'd *been sleeping* for more than an hour when a scary nightmare woke me up.
> Grandpa *had been smoking* cigars for almost fifty years when he suddenly gave them up.

2. To form the past perfect continuous tense, we use *had* and *been* as auxiliaries and a present participle as a main verb. *Not* follows *had* in negative verb phrases:

	singular		**plural**	
1st person	I		we	
2nd person	you	had (not) been doing	you	had (not) been doing
3rd person	he		they	
	she			
	it			

3. Adverbs like *just, never, recently,* and *finally* sometimes occur with the past perfect tense. They follow *had:*

> I'd *just* been talking to Mr. Towers when he suddenly fainted.
> He'd *recently* been working for that company when it went out of business.

When no adverbs are present in a verb phrase, adverbial expressions of time nearly always appear in sentences in the past perfect continuous tense:

When we finally got to Tibet, we'd been traveling *for a month.*
Grandma had been working *for sixty-three* years when she finally retired.

4. When the past perfect tense occurs in a complex sentence, adverbs of time like *yesterday, last night,* and *ago* must usually take a different form in order to keep the sentence logical:

(*yesterday*) When I first met her, she'd just arrived in this country *the day before.*
(*last night*) I was tired when I woke up on Sunday morning because I'd stayed up too late *the night before.*
(*ago*) When the nurse gave me a shot, she'd already given me one an hour *before.*

120 the past perfect tense with *yet*

1. In sentences with the past perfect tense, the adverb *yet* is most often found in its usual position at the end of a subordinate or main clause containing a verb phrase in its negative form:

I *hadn't learned* how to speak *yet* when I was a year old.
We were all laughing hard even though Daniel *hadn't finished* his joke *yet.*

We sometimes also find *yet* following *had not* (*hadn't*) in more formal usage:

When Edison was thirty, he *had not yet* invented the phonograph.
It was two minutes before curtain time, and the leading actress *hadn't yet* made up.

2. When a negative word occurs in a subject, *yet* may follow an affirmative verb phrase:

The teacher was worried because *none* of the students *had come* to class *yet.*

In such sentences, *yet* may appear within a verb phrase:

The teacher was annoyed because not one member of the class *had yet* done any homework, and it was almost the fifth week of the semester.

3. In rather formal usage, the verbal phrase *had yet* + an infinitive sometimes occurs:

After being in Cairo for almost six weeks, they *had yet to pay* a visit to the pyramids.

121 questions with the past perfect (continuous) tense

1. In yes–no and information questions in the past perfect (continuous) tense, the subject of a sentence follows the auxiliary *had:*

> *Had you* had your breakfast when you left the house this morning? No, I hadn't.
> *Had the patient* been having pains in his side for a long time when he finally decided to go to the doctor? Yes, he had (been).
> Where else *had you* studied English before you came to this school?
> How long *had your brother* been studying at the university before he found out what he wanted to do in the world when he finally graduated?

2. Adverbs follow the subject:

> Had *you already* made your decision when the committee asked for it? No, I hadn't.
> Had *you just* been speaking to Jim on the other line when I called you up? Yes, I had (been).

3. We may observe either a formal or informal style in negative questions:

> **formal:**
> *Had you not* yet made up your mind when you were asked to give a decision?
> *Had the student not* been cheating for several weeks when the teacher eventually caught her copying out of the answer book?
> For how long *had you not* been working when you finally went back to work?

> **informal:**
> *Hadn't you* had your lunch yet when you went back to the office?
> *Hadn't you* been having a good time when you left the party so early?
> Why *hadn't you* gotten up yet when breakfast was being served downstairs in the dining room?

Pronunciation note: *Hadn't you* most often sounds like *hadn't-chew.*

Note: Questions containing the past perfect tense usually appear in rather formal usage. It is easier for a speaker to use the simple past tense in a main clause combined with the simple past tense in a subordinate clause introduced by *before:*

> *Did* you *have* your breakfast before you left the house this morning?
> Why *didn't* he *go* to his lawyer before he invested all his money in that foolish speculation?

4. Because the past perfect tense always expresses an event before an event, the form is most often present in a clause accompanied by another clause containing a verb in the simple past tense. This other clause (either main or subordinate) may be expressed or understood:

> What was your roommate doing when you got home last night? (When I *got* home last night,) . . . she'*d already gone* to bed.
> Why were you so tired the other morning? (I was tired the other morning) . . . because I *hadn't slept* well the night before.

122   lay and lie

1. You will recall that verbs that may take direct objects are called TRANSITIVE:

> The delivery boy *put the groceries* in the refrigerator for me.
> You *left your keys* on the hall table, didn't you?

and verbs that cannot take direct objects are called INTRANSITIVE:

> Hurricanes rarely *occur* in this part of the country, fortunately.
> Many different kinds of characters *appear* in Shakespeare's plays.

2. The irregular verb *lie* (*lay, lain, lying*) is intransitive; it cannot take a direct object. The verb can mean to recline or be in a reclining or horizontal position:

> Jeff, Kathleen *has just lain down* for a nap, so please turn your radio down.
> Someone's money *is lying* on the coffee table in the living room.
> Yes, many, many problems *lie* on the shoulders of the Prime Minister.
> The gangsters *lay* low (hid) in an abandoned garage until things cooled off.

3. The regular verb *lie* (*lied, lied, lying*) means not to tell the truth; in other words, to tell a lie or make up a story. Like the irregular verb *lie*, it is intransitive:

> Since she's *always lying,* people no longer believe anything she says.
> "How dare you *lie* to me," she said to him in a fit of anger.

4. The irregular verb *lay* (*laid, laid, laying*) is transitive; it may take a direct object:

> How many eggs a day does a chicken usually *lay?*
> Why are you *laying* those packages on the kitchen table?
> When I last looked into the chicken coop, not one hen *had laid* an egg yet.
> Who *laid* her shoes on my bed?

123 set and sit

1. The irregular verb *set* (*set, set, setting*) is intransitive; it can mean *to lower* (most often in reference to the sun):

> The sun *has set*, and the evening has finally begun.
> The closer you get to the Equator, the more quickly the sun *sets*.

2. *Set* can also mean to harden or solidfy:

> We poured the concrete at least ten hours ago; I'm sure that it's *already set*.
> I made some Jello a few minutes ago; it *hasn't set* yet.

3. *Set* occurs as a transitive verb when it means to arrange, place, or put in a specified place:

> She *set* the table with some lovely silverware she'd inherited from her grandmother.
> The jeweler *set* the diamond in a beautiful gold ring.
> My roommate *sets* her hair every night before she goes to bed.

4. The irregular verb *sit* (*sat, sat, sitting*) is intransitive; it means to rest with the torso (body) in a vertical position:

> Young man, do you realize you're *sitting* in my favorite chair?
> I've just got to *sit down*; I've been standing up on my feet all day.

124 raise and rise

1. The regular verb *raise* (*raised, raised, raising*) is transitive; it always takes a direct object. It means to move or cause to move upward:

> Would you please *raise* the window; it's getting a little warm in here.
> What wonderful vegetables you're *raising* in the garden!
> His parents died in a flu epidemic when Robert was very young; his aunt and uncle, on his mother's side, *raised* (reared) him.

2. The irregular verb *rise* (*rose, risen, rising*) is intransitive; it never takes an object. It means to ascend or move from a lower to a higher position:

> It was strange when, all by itself, the window suddenly *rose*.
> The sun *has risen*, but most everyone in town is still sleeping.

125 the passive voice

1. A verb phrase may be in the *active* or *passive voice.*

active: The woman *bore* her child easily.
passive: The child *was born* easily.

2. In the active voice, the subject of the sentence is the *"doer"* of the action; the subject itself generates the action:

The pitcher (subject and doer) *threw* the ball to the catcher.
The catcher (subject and doer) *caught* the ball.

3. A passive verb indicates that the subject of the sentence is the *receiver* of the action generated by the verb:

The ball (receiver) *was thrown* to the catcher.
The ball (receiver) *was caught.*

4. In the passive voice, we use a form of the verb *be* (as an auxiliary) and a past participle (as a main verb).

    a. Present Tense: Hundreds of thousands of books *are published* every year.

    b. Past Tense: My mother *was introduced* to my father at her aunt's house.

    c. Future Tense: You *will be given* your diploma at the graduation ceremonies.

    d. Present Perfect Tense: Many things *have been discussed* in the class.

    e. Past Perfect Tense: By the end of the day nothing *had been done.*

5. Only transitive verbs may be used in the passive voice. Compare how transitive verbs in the passive voice may be transformed into passive verb phrases:

active	*passive*
Someone set *the table* (direct object).	*The table* (subject) was set.
Someone raised *the window.*	*The window* was raised.
They laid *the plans.*	*The plans* were laid.

6. Intransitive verbs cannot be used in the passive voice because they cannot take a direct or an indirect object:

Why are you *sitting?* Why are you *lying?* How quickly the sun is *rising!*

7. Like a direct object, an indirect object of an active verb can become the subject of a sentence when the verb phrase is transformed into the passive voice:

I gave *him* (indirect object) the news. = *He* (subject) was given the news (by me).
I made *them* (indirect object) a proposal. = *They* (subject) were made a proposal (by me).

The direct objects in the above examples can also become subjects:

The news was given to them.
A proposal was made to them.

8. In negative verb phrases, the adverb *not* is placed after the initial verb or auxiliary in a phrase:

When the lawn *isn't* watered every day, it gets brown and dry.
He *wasn't given* a promotion because he'd insulted the boss.
Dinner *won't be served* until the last guest arrives.
The hostages *haven't* been released yet.
Their baby boy was almost a week old, but he *hadn't* been named yet.

126   the passive voice with adverbs

1. Adverbs follow the initial verb or auxiliary in a passive verb phrase:

The refrigerator *is always* cleaned out once a month.
Our children *were never* spoiled when they were young.
A Democrat *will probably* be elected in the next election.
At last! Peace *has finally* been found.
When we arrived in the country, diplomatic relations with the United States *had just* been broken.

2. The active voice is more frequently used than the passive; it is generally felt by most writers that the active voice is more direct and effective. However, the passive voice is preferred in the following cases:

a. When we do not know who performed the action:

A million dollars *was robbed* from that bank yesterday afternoon.
Look! The letter I just got out of the mailbox *has already been opened* by someone.

b. When we wish to draw attention to the receiver of the action:

My watch was made in Switzerland. (We would seldom say *People made* . . . .)
He was born at home. (It would be unusual to say *His mother bore* . . .)

c. When it is desirable to maintain an impersonal tone, as in textbooks, in technical or scientific writing, in newspaper reporting, and in the language of diplomacy and the law:

The results of the tests *have been carefully studied.*
Textbooks *are usually written* by teachers.

127 transforming active verb phrases into passive verb phrases

1. When a passive verb phrase is used in a sentence, the *performing agent* (doer) is often not mentioned:

The mail *is delivered* every day except Sunday.
The garbage *is picked up* every other day.

or not known:

A child in my neighborhood *has recently been kidnapped.*
My car *has just been stolen.*

2. When the performing agent is mentioned, it follows the verb phrase and is introduced by the preposition *by:*

Romeo and Juliet was written *by William Shakespeare.*
This rug was made *by Navajo Indians* on their reservation in the state of New Mexico.

128 the present continuous tense and the passive voice

In passive verb phrases containing the present continuous tense, we use a form of the verb *be* as the first auxiliary, the *-ing* form of the verb *be* as the second auxiliary, and a past participle as the main verb of the phrase:

They're certain their letters *are being censored.*
They're *being married* in a civil ceremony.

The adverb *not* follows the first auxiliary:

I want to speak to the manager; I'm *not being served* properly.
Even though he *isn't being paid* much, he enjoys working at his company.

129 the past continuous tense and the passive voice

In the passive voice, the past continuous tense follows the same pattern as the present continuous tense:

While Berlin *was being destroyed,* Hitler committed suicide.
They *were being paid* by their government while they were studying.

I *wasn't being told* a fish story when I was told that, was I?
You *weren't being cheated* when you signed that contract, were you?

130   yes-no questions in the passive voice

In a yes–no question, the subject of a sentence is put after the initial auxiliary in a passive verb phrase:

Are you often given promotions in your company?
Was your package delivered yesterday on time?
Will our apartment ever be painted?
Has your teenager ever been taken out on a date?
Had the guest of honor already been introduced to everyone when you arrived at the reception?

131   information questions in the passive voice

1. In an information question, the subject is put after the initial auxiliary in a passive verb phrase:

How often *is the garbage* picked up in your neighborhood?
Why *are your neighbors* being arrested?
How *was the problem* eventually solved?
Who *were you* being introduced to when I saw you across the room?
Where *have the aspirins* been put?
Why *had you* been promoted even though you and your boss didn't get along?

2. As with sentences containing active verb phrases, when an information word(s) is the subject of a sentence, the usual question form is not used:

What *has been done* about the inadequate water supply in our town?
Who in this class *had already studied* English before they started this course?

132   passive versus active verb phrases

1. A common mistake for students to make is to use an intransitive verb in a passive verb phrase. Compare:

correct	**incorrect**
The patient *died* suddenly.	The patient [was died] suddenly.
He *appeared* on TV.	He [was appeared] on TV.

2. With the verb *sell* (in reference to a company or a store's sales), the active or passive voice may be interchangeable:

A million copies of that book *have sold* (*have been sold*) since its publication.

I wanted to buy one of them yesterday at the store, but they'd already *sold out* (*been sold out*).

133 passive infinitives

To be + a past participle forms a passive infinitive:

Miss, I'd like these dishes *to be cleared away*, please.

Would you like this coffee *to be ground up*, Madame?

No one likes *to be thrown out of* a place.

134 the future perfect tense

1. *Will* (*shall*) + *have* + a past participle (as a main verb) are used to form a verb phrase in the FUTURE PERFECT TENSE. In the passive voice, the auxiliary verb *been* follows *have*:

	singular		*plural*	
1st person	I		we	
2nd person	you	will have	you	will have
3rd person	he	(been) done	they	(been) done
	she			
	it			

Reminder: *Shall* in first person occurs most frequently in British English.

2. The future perfect tense is used for an event that precedes another in the future:

The world *will have become* an even smaller place when we enter the twenty-first century.

The stars *will have come out* when we've finished supper—we can go out and look for constellations.

The form is also used to express the duration of an event prior to another in the future:

When we arrive at Sydney, we *will have been* on this ship for more than a month; it's been a long voyage from Rio de Janeiro.

We'll *have been* on this plane for eleven hours when we get to Buenos Aires.

It may also be used for repeated events:

> By the end of the day, many things *will have been done* in this office, but nothing will have been accomplished—the whole place must be reorganized.
>
> The world *will have seen* many changes take place before we've entered the new millennium.

3. The adverb *not* follows *will* in a negative verb phrase:

> In the year 2000, our daughter *won't* have graduated from college yet. Because of the problem of overpopulation, by the end of the twentieth century, many countries in the developing world *will not* have made as much progress as they should have.

4. The adverb *already* often occurs in the future perfect tense and is usually found following *will* in a verb phrase:

> By the middle of next semester, we *will already* have done approximately 150 quizzes.

However, it can also be placed after *have:*

> We hope that when the world finally runs out of oil, an inexpensive and effective substitute will *have already* been found.

The adverb *probably* may precede or follow *will*—*probably* and *already* make frequent appearances together in a verb phrase:

> By my calculations, we *probably will* have *already* sighted land by early morning—we're getting close to the coast.
>
> The children *will probably already* have done their chores by the time the sun has set.

5. The future perfect tense is most often accompanied by a time clause beginning with *when*, or by time expressions with a preposition like *on*, *at*, or *by:*

> *When we celebrate our golden anniversary next week*, my wife and I *will have known* each other fifty-three years.
>
> *On July 4, 2000*, the United States *will have been* independent from Great Britain for 223 years.

> **Note:** The future perfect tense (particularly its continuous form) does not occur so frequently as the other verb tenses.

135 the future perfect continuous tense

For the FUTURE PERFECT CONTINUOUS TENSE, *will* (*shall*) *have been* + a present participle is used to form a verb phrase. We use this tense to emphasize the duration of an event prior to another in the future:

By the time the monsoon finally comes to an end in late August, it *will have been* raining off and on for approximately three and a half months.

When our son gets home from his travels this time, he *will have been running around* the world for more than five years—he's got to settle down now.

136 questions with the future perfect (continuous) tense

1. In yes–no and information questions with the future perfect (continuous) tense, the subject usually follows *will* (*shall*) except when an information word is the subject of a question:

> *Will this plan* have been approved by the committee by tomorrow?
> How long *will the two of you* have been going together when you finally get married next week?
> *What will* have happened to the world by the year 5000?

2. We may include *have* in yes–no answers, but its use is optional:

> Will you have been here a long time by then?
> Yes, I will (have).   No, I won't (have).

137 modal auxiliaries; *can*

1. Modal auxiliaries constitute a group of words which add a special meaning to the verbs that they precede. The following chart contains a list of the modal auxiliaries and their contracted and noncontracted negative forms.

	noncontracted negative form	*contracted negative form*
can	cannot, can not	can't
could	could not	couldn't
may	may not	mayn't (British)
might	might not	mightn't (British)
shall	shall not	shan't (British)
should (ought to)	should not (ought not to)	shouldn't (oughtn't to)
will ('ll)	will not ('ll not)	won't
would ('d)	would not ('d not)	wouldn't
must	must not	mustn't
need	need not	needn't
dare	dare not	daren't (British)

2. A base form always follows a modal auxiliary in either the active or passive voice:

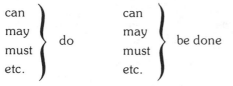

3. Adverbs usually follow modals:

> Grandpa *can still* run fast.
> The soprano *might never* sing again.

or they may sometimes precede modals:

> You *always must* obey your conscience.
> You *never could* work a miracle.

Adverbs follow *not* in negative verb phrases:

> We shouldn*'t ever* be cruel to animals.
> He *can't always* depend on his roommate.

and they most often follow subjects in questions:

> Must *we always* have war?
> Can *people never* get along with each other?

4. The modal auxiliary *can* + a base form expresses ability or possibility:

> No one in the gym *can lift* so many weights as Mr. Atlas.
> Boris *can speak* five languages, but not one can he speak well.
> Not a soul *can be found* on the streets in my town on early Sunday morning.

5. When expressing possibility, *can* may indicate future time:

> No decision can be announced to the press *until one has been made.*
> We can take a break *as soon as we finish the next quiz.*

6. *Can not* usually appears as *cannot*. *Can't*, the contraction of *cannot*, occurs in informal usage:

> You can lead a horse to water, but you *can't* make him drink. (old saying)
> You *can't* teach an old dog new tricks. (old saying)

Pronunciation note: The vowel in *can* is usually unstressed; for example, *I can* sounds like *I-kin; he can* sounds like *he-kin.* However, there is a stress on *can* when we want emphasis:

She can't sing well, but *he can* (not *he-kin*).

The vowel in *can't* is given its full value. With the help of your teacher, practice reading the following sentences aloud.

I *can* dance well, but my sister *can't.* I *can't* sing, and neither *can* she.
No one *can* do anything as well as I *can.* I *can* even work miracles.
She *can't* figure it out, but *he can,* and so *can I.*
We *can* hit better than *they can,* but *they can* catch better than *we can.*

138 questions with *can*

1. In yes–no and information questions, *can* precedes the subject in all persons:

Can horses run as fast as lions?
How many eggs a day *can a hen* lay?

Can follows a subject when the subject occurs as an information word:

What can be done about the spiders in the linen closet?
Who in this class *can* stay under water for more than five minutes?

2. In informal usage, a subject follows *can't* in negative questions:

Can't you be still? *Can't we* kiss and make up?

Pronunciation note: *Can't you* most often sounds like *can't-chew.*

The subject follows *can* in formal usage:

Why, Professor, *can this antique vase* not be duplicated easily?
General, *can the people* not be trusted to vote for the right person in the next election?

3. *Can* occurs in short yes–no answers:

Can you help me out? Yes, I *can.* No, I *can't.*
Can it be done today? Yes, it *can* (be). No, it *can't* (be).

139 *could*

Could, the past form of *can,* expresses ability and possibility in past time:

We *could enter* the theater without paying—there was no one at the door.
We *couldn't* (could not) *take* the elevator up to the 99th floor (the power had gone off), so *we* had to walk up.

140   be able to

1. Essentially, the idiom *be able to* + a base form has the same meaning as the modal auxiliary *can:*

> I'm *able to* (can) write well with my left hand as well as my right.
> I *wasn't able to* (couldn't) follow the speaker's talk (speech); he wasn't able to convey his ideas in words.

2. *Be able to* may occur in all the six verb tenses:

> Rarely *am* I ever *able to* get up easily in the mornings.
> The climbers *were able to* reach the top of the mountain, but because of the sudden storm, they weren't able to come down—they had to be rescued by helicopters.
> I haven't got enough credits; I *won't be able to* graduate this coming June.
> *Have* you ever *been able to* understand Shakespeare's plays?
> Never *had* I really *been able to* enjoy the work of Charles Dickens until I went to England and visited the places he'd described so beautifully in his novels.
> Yes, Sir, by the year 2000, we'll *have been able to* pay back this loan to the bank.

141   *could have;* **past opportunity not realized**

Could have + (been) + a past participle is used to express *past opportunity not realized:*

> The Duke of Windsor *could have remained* (was able to remain) on the throne as the King of England for his whole life, but he wanted to marry Wallace Simpson, the woman he loved.
> Yes, our house *could have been painted* white, but we eventually decided on red instead.

> **Note:** The adverb *instead* often occurs in such sentences with *could have.*

> **Pronunciation note:** *Could have* usually sounds like *could-of.*

142   *could, could have;* **probability and conjecture**

1. Besides being used to express ability and possibility in past time, *could* may be used to express *probability* in present time:

Yes, boys and girls, I *could work* a miracle for you (it's probable), but I haven't got my magic book with me.

Could also expresses conjecture (guessing) in present time:

Why isn't Pete Stark pitching today? His arm *could be* on the blink (injured)—who knows?

2. *Could have* + (*been*) + a past participle is used to express probability and conjecture in past time:

Why is Connie no longer coming to school? She *could have dropped out;* she was having some difficulties at home.
Why is this meat so tender? It *could have been cooked* with a tenderizer.

Pronunciation reminder: *Could have* most often sounds like *could-of.*

143 *couldn't have;* impossibility

1. *Couldn't* is used to express the *lack* of ability or *no* possibility in past time:

Since the gas tank was empty, we *couldn't* (weren't able to) start the car.
The beach was so crowded, we *couldn't* (weren't able to) find a place to lie down.

We also use *couldn't* to express impossibility in the *present:*

It's impossible! I *couldn't* finish all this work in one day, Sir; I've got only two hands.
K.C. Peters *couldn't* know much about Australia; he's never been there.

2. *Couldn't have* + (*been*) + a past participle expresses impossibility in past time:

Your Honor, that crime *couldn't have been committed* by me; I've got an alibi. I was home with my mother at the time.
Bob and Alice, thank you so much; your party *couldn't have been* more delightful. We had a perfectly wonderful time.

Pronunciation note: Usually, *couldn't have* sounds like *couldn't-of.*

144   questions with *could have*

1. In yes–no and information questions with *could have,* the subject usually occurs after *could:*

> I can't find my shoes. *Could they* have been thrown away by mistake?
> Betty Drew, how *could you* have made such a rude remark to your mother?

However, *could* follows subjects that are information words:

> *What could* have happened in that accident? Was the man pushed, or did he fall?
> *Who could* have sung *Tosca* more beautifully than Madame Callas?

2. In yes–no answers, *have* may follow the modal, but its use is optional:

> Could your mother and father ever have considered leaving this city for good?
> Yes, they *could* (*have*)—it's probable. No, they *couldn't* (*have*)—it's impossible.

3. *Couldn't have* often occurs in questions; a subject follows *couldn't:*

> *Couldn't you* have been earlier? Why *couldn't you* have gotten here on time?

In formal usage, the subject follows *could:*

> *Could you* not have been at my side during the recent crisis, son?
> Why *could the leftist students* not have been released from prison?

> **Pronunciation note:** *Could* I (you, he, she, it, we, they) *have* most often sounds like *could* I (you, etc.) *-of; could you have* sounds similar to *could-jew-of,* and *couldn't you have* sounds like *couldn't-chew-of.*

145   asking for permission with *may* and *can*

1. In formal usage, the modal auxiliary *may* is used to ask for permission. *Can* is heard in less formal speech:

> *May* I introduce you to Professor Howitzer, the distinguished physicist?
> *Can* I play fullback in the next quarter, Coach?

2. A request for permission takes the form of a yes–no question, and a yes–no answer grants or denies the permission. **Second person** (singular or plural) **does not occur in a request for permission.**

1st person	May (can) I help you?	Yes, you may (can).
	May (can) we leave now?	No, you may not
		(cannot, can't).
3rd person	May (can) he hunt here?	Yes, he may (can).
	May (can) they dance here?	No, they may not
		(cannot, can't).

Note: *Mayn't,* the contraction of *may not,* occurs only in British usage.

3. *May* and *can* are also used to mean *be permitted:*

We *may use* (are permitted to use) our dictionaries during the examination.

People *cannot* smoke (are not permitted to smoke) in elevators.

4. The polite word *please* is best used in a request for permission; it follows the subject:

May *I please* leave the room? Can *we please* park our car here?

5. *Could* sometimes occurs in requests for permission; however, *can* or *may* usually appears in the answer:

Could I please ask you a personal question? Yes, you *may.* No, you *cannot.*

6. The modal auxiliary *might,* another form of *may,* occasionally appears in a request for permission, but it is very formal and is rarely heard in informal speech:

Might I leave my calling card? *Might* we draw this meeting to a close?

7. Both *may* and *can* sometimes occur in requests that are not asking for permission. This kind of request is similar in meaning to requests in the imperative mood:

Waiter, may I please have a fork? (Please give me a fork.)
Can we please have our tickets? (Please give us our tickets.)

Second person may occur in the form:

Could you please give me change? (Please give me change.)

146   *may* and *might;* conjecture

1. Besides asking for permission and making requests, *may,* and its other form *might,* are used to express conjecture. Essentially, *may* and *might* have the same meaning:

The world *may* (might) blow itself up someday with the way things are going.

2. A statement with *may* or *might* is made in response to some kind of evidence known by the speaker. Compare:

evidence	*conjecture*
She's always very quiet.	She *may have* a great many secrets.
Doesn't this salad taste bland?	Yes, it *might not have* any salt in it.
How foolishly he's acting!	He *might be* in love.

Note: *Mightn't*, the contraction of *might not*, is chiefly British.

3. Do not confuse the adverb *maybe*, a synonym for *perhaps*, with *may be*. *Maybe* usually occurs at the beginning of a sentence; *may be* always follows the subject:

Why is the baby crying? *Maybe* she's hungry. She *may be* hungry.

147   *may have* and *might have;* conjecture about the past

May have or *might have* + (been) + a past participle is used to express conjecture about an event in either present or past time:

event	*conjecture*
Why is he sneezing so much?	He *may have caught* a cold.
Why did they get lost?	They *might have been given* the wrong directions.

Pronunciation note: *May have* or *might have* sounds like *may-of* or *might-of*, *may not have* sounds like *may-not-of*, and *might not have* sounds like *might-not-of*.

148   *may have* and *might have; that* noun clauses

1. *May* does not occur in questions about conjecture (only in requests). In very formal usage, *might* or *might have* occurs, but they are not often heard in informal speech.

Secrets are leaking out. *Might* there *be* a spy in the president's office?
I didn't get the letter. *Might* it *not have been sent?*

2. Because past forms of modal auxiliaries like *could* and *might* are usually quite formal and awkward to use in direct question forms (and since *may* has no question form except in requests), they most often occur in *that* noun clauses following such verbs as *think* and *feel*. *That* may be omitted in a sentence:

> Do you think (that) I *might have been double-crossed* by my partner?
> Does the boss think (that) we *could have done* the project more quickly?
> Do you feel (that) we *may have ended up* in the wrong place?

149 *must;* **necessity, prohibition, deduction, and recommendation**

1. The modal auxiliary *must* + a base form may express:

a. Necessity: The world *must be* made a better place than it is.
b. Prohibition: We *must not forget* to stand up for our rights.
c. Deduction: It *must be* exciting to stand at the summit of Mt. Everest.
d. Recommendation: You *must read* this book—it's about you.

2. As with *may,* a deduction made with *must* is made in response to some kind of evidence that is known to the speaker. But *must* shows a stronger sense of certainty and probability than *may;* there is no conjecture. Compare:

evidence	*deduction*
Singapore is on the other side of the globe from New York.	It *must take* a long time to get there on a ship.
That's a big elephant, isn't it?	Yes, it *must weigh* much more than a ton.

3. We use *mustn't,* the contraction of *must not,* in informal usage:

> I have a fever and no appetite. I *mustn't* be well.
> No one is going to that movie. It *mustn't* be any good.

However, *mustn't* is most often used for prohibition:

> This is confidential information—it *mustn't* be revealed to anyone.

Must not occurs more frequently for deduction, even in informal speaking:

> This safe just won't open. You *must not* have the right combination.

4. We may ask questions with *must* when the modal expresses necessity:

> *Must we* leave now? Yes, you must. No, you mustn't.
> *Must this* be done now? Yes, it must (be). No, it mustn't (be).

When *must* expresses deduction, however, there is no question form.

150 *must have;* deduction

1. *Must* may be used to express necessity and prohibition in present and future time only:

> We *must listen* to our conscience; we *mustn't give in* to temptation.
> This job *mustn't be put off* until tomorrow; it *must be* finished at once.

2. However, we show deduction in past time with *must have* + (*been*) + a past participle:

> How beautiful life *must have been* in ancient Greece!
> Yes, I've been around the world ten times. You *must have seen* and *done* a lot.

3. *Not* follows *must* in negative verb phrases:

> It *must not* have been easy for Christopher Columbus and his crew to set out on their voyage to the New World—their destination was unknown.
> This silver is still tarnished; it *mustn't* have been polished enough.

> **Reminder:** No question form occurs when we use *must* for deduction.
>
> **Pronunciation note:** *Must have* sounds like *must-of* and *mustn't have* sounds like *mustn't-of.*

151 the idiom *have to;* necessity and lack of necessity

1. Like *must,* the idiom *have (has) to* + a base form expresses necessity:

> Most of us *have to* (*must*) *work* for a living.
> The First Secretary *has to* (*must*) *be* given this message right away.

> **Pronunciation note:** *Have to* sounds like *half-to.* The idiom has a different pronunciation from *have* meaning possession.

2. Negative verb phrases with *have to* express *lack of necessity.* We always use *do, does,* or *did* + *not* in negative verb phrases with *have to* in the present and past tenses:

> These letters *don't have to be mailed*—I'll deliver them by hand myself.
> This is an excellent composition, Cynthia—it *doesn't have to be done* over.
> No, there weren't any difficulties—the boss *didn't have to be called.*

3. *Do, does,* or *did* always occurs in questions with *have to* in the present and past tenses:

> *Do* you *have to* study a great deal? Yes, I do. No, I don't.
> *Does* this *have to* be mended? Yes, it does. No, it doesn't.
> Why *did* they *have to* go to the bank? They'd run out of money.

Note: The auxiliary *do* occurs in questions and negatives containing *have to* in both American and British usage.

152 *must not* versus *do not have to;* prohibition versus lack of necessity

1. Essentially, *have to* and *must* are similar in meaning:

> How fast the person in the token booth *has to* (*must*) make change!
> All of us *have to* (*must*) think about the future even though it does seem far away.

Have to does not express necessity so strongly as *must* does. Besides necessity and prohibition, *must* may convey a feeling of strong obligation or loyalty:

> We *must believe* that all people are created equal in the eyes of God.
> Fellow citizens, we *must defend* our country against these evil invaders on our native soil.

Have to is most often related to the problems of daily living:

> My birds *have to be fed* twice a day.
> She *has to wind* her watch every day.

2. However, the negative form of *have to* has a completely different meaning from the negative form of *must*. *Must not* means prohibition, but *do not have to* means lack of necessity. Compare:

prohibition	*lack of necessity*
We *must not* steal.	He *doesn't have to steal* anything—he's able to do business in an honest way.
We *must not* kill.	I *don't have to* kill those flies lying on the floor; they're already dead.
We *must not* lie.	Our company *doesn't have to* lie in its advertising—we've got a good product.

153 *have to;* contrasting verb tenses

Like the idiom *be able to, have to* can be used in all the verb tenses:

Never does my sister *have to* do so many chores as I do; it's not fair.

Nothing *had to* be done to our new house before we moved in; it was in perfect condition.

Even though we *will have to* spend a lot of money, we want to give our daughter a beautiful wedding. It will be a once-in-a-lifetime occasion, we hope.

My boss and I *have had to* have some very important meetings this week.

No, the patient wasn't able to leave the hospital at that time because he *had* just *had to* have a second operation.

When you arrive at around midnight, we *will have* already *had to* leave.

154 *should* and *ought to;* advisability, expectation, obligation, and recommendation

1. The modal *should* has exactly the same meaning as the modal *ought to:*

The people in this country *should (ought to)* learn more about people in other parts of the world.

In American English, however, *should* occurs more frequently than *ought to.*

2. *Should* or *ought to* expresses:

a. Advisability: You really *ought to lie down* and rest—you look worn out.

b. Expectation: Children *should be seen* and not heard. (old saying)

c. Obligation: Everyone *ought to work* for world peace.

d. Recommendation: You *should find* an English-speaking roommate; it will help to improve your conversation, and you may find it an educational experience.

Pronunciation note: When speaking quickly, *ought to* sometimes sounds like *ought-a.*

3. We insert *not* between *should* and a base form. We use the contraction *shouldn't* in less formal usage:

The rich and the powerful *should not oppress* the poor and the weak.

Please stop gossiping, Meredith; we *shouldn't talk* about people behind their backs.

4. *Not* is inserted between *ought* and *to*. *Oughtn't,* the contraction of *ought not,* is chiefly British and is not commonly heard in American English.

> Sandy, you *ought not to* read over my shoulder; it's rather rude.
> You *oughtn't to* miss the Tower of London while you're on your tour of the city; you can send post cards from there to America.

5. The expectation or advisability expressed with *should* or *ought to* is very weak:

> Class, homework assignments and compositions *should be done* as neatly as possible, but some of you have been getting a little sloppy lately.
> The streets in this part of the city *ought to be cleaned* twice a day, but we're lucky if they're cleaned once a week.

6. Like *must,* the word *should* or *ought to* is used to show a kind of obligation or sense of necessity, but there is a difference in meaning. Compare:

> You *shouldn't smoke;* it's a dirty habit.
>
> Someone *ought to take care of* those plants; they're dying.

> You *mustn't smoke;* you're killing yourself.
>
> You *must take care of* your health; you're not getting any younger.

7. Recommendations with *should* and *ought to* also have less force than those made with *must.* Compare:

> You *ought to read* this book; it might interest you.
>
> I *should buy* this cereal; someone told me it was good for the price.

> You *must read* this book; it will tell you how to become a millionaire in twenty easy lessons.
>
> You *must buy* this cereal; it will make your children grow taller, stronger, and more intelligent.

155 *should have* and *ought to have;* advisability and obligation in the past

Should have (*ought to have*) + (*been*) + a past participle is used to express advisability and obligation in past time. It is understood that the advice was not followed or the obligation was not fulfilled:

> This blouse *should have been washed* in cool water, but it wasn't and it shrank.

The baby *should have had* a nap this afternoon—she's tired and irritable this evening.

You *ought to have slept* more last night, but you didn't, and now you're too tired to study this morning.

I *ought not to have been* so rude to my guests, but their foolish opinions made me so angry that I kicked them out of the house.

Pronunciation note: *Should have* sounds like *should-of, shouldn't have* sounds like *shouldn't-of, ought to have* sounds like *ought-to-of*, and *ought not to have* sounds like *ought-not-to-of*.

156   questions with *should* and *should have*

1. Subjects follow *should* in yes–no and information questions:

Should this be done now? How *should it* have been done the first time?

except when an information word is the subject:

What should be done tomorrow? *Who should* have done it yesterday?

Pronunciation note: *Should I* (you, etc.) *have* sounds like *should-I-of*.

2. In yes–no answers, *be* may follow *should,* but its use is optional:

Should it *be* done this way? Yes, it should (be). No, it shouldn't (be).

Have or *have + been* may also follow *should* in yes–no answers:

Should I *have* done it? Yes, you should (have). No, you shouldn't (have).

Should it have been done? Yes, it should have (been). No, it shouldn't have (been).

Note: Questions with *ought to* are almost never heard in American English.

157   *should* and *should have* with *have to*

The idiom *have to* sometimes occurs with the modal *should.* Most often, the verb phrase is in its negative form:

You *shouldn't have to pick up* the mail at the post office yourself. Don't you have a mailman who delivers it every day?

The boss wants us to be at the meeting at eight, but we *shouldn't have to be* there so early—it's not necessary.

What a foolish waste of money! They *shouldn't have had to spend*

$100,000 to have a nice wedding for their daughter. They were just showing off.

We *shouldn't have had to pay* so much to get from the airport to the hotel; I think we were being ripped off (cheated) by some crooked (dishonest) cab driver.

158 *should* and *should have* with *be able to*

The idiom *be able to* also makes an occasional appearance with *should,* in either affirmative or negative verb phrases:

Helmut *should be able to learn* English quickly (he already speaks five languages), but he's not making much progress.

She always gets to work late; she *shouldn't be able to get away with* it.

What! You *should have been able* to buy a good pair of shoes without paying $400. You must be made of money.

Those people *shouldn't have been able to enter* this contest—they're not eligible.

159 *must* and *must have* with *have to*

Have to may occasionally appear with *must* and *must have* in either affirmative or negative verb phrases:

What a difficult and dangerous job he has! Yes, he *must have to work* very hard, but he's making good money, isn't he?

What a lazy life Wanda Richhouse leads! Yes, she *mustn't ever have to do* anything except have a good time. How boring!

I hear your neighbors next door have recently sold their house. Yes, they *must have had to sell* it; they both lost their jobs a couple of months ago.

It wasn't always so easy teaching in junior high school. I can imagine. You *must have had to have* a lot of patience and understanding—I could never have done it myself.

Note: Once in a while, *may* or *might* also appears with *have to:*

The power hasn't come back on yet— we *may have to use* candles this evening. Have we got any?

Why is Mother late this evening? She *may have had to run* a few errands.

160   *must* and *must have* with *be able to*

From time to time, *be able to* joins with *must* and *must have*:

Sir, I *must be able to get on* the next plane for Riyadh; I've got an extremely important meeting there at nine tomorrow morning.

The man has put an X on the dotted line at the bottom of the contract with the landlord; he *must not be able to read* and write.

She seems extremely upset, doesn't she? Yes, she *mustn't have been able to get* a visa to visit her son, who is in prison somewhere in the Soviet Union.

Bob Gordon looks like a new man, doesn't he? Yes, he *must finally have been able to make* a date with the new student in chemistry lab; he's been talking about her for weeks.

Note: *May* or *might* also occurs with *be able to* on occasion:

Betsy, you *might be able to climb up* to the top of the tree, but are you going to be able to climb down safely?

Frank and Helen *may have been able to spend* a lot of money on their daughter's wedding, but they weren't able to find the groom, who never showed up.

161   modals and present continuous forms

1. *Be* + a present participle follows a modal in a present continuous form:

Come on, everyone, we *should be setting* off for our next camp. We've got a full day's hike ahead of us.

Excuse me, Sir, you *ought not to be sitting* in the waiting room; it's reserved for women and children.

You *must be kidding.* This isn't a diamond, it's only glass.

2. Subjects follow the modal in yes–no and information questions:

Ladies and Gentlemen, *must we* always be arguing among ourselves? We must come to a consensus.

3. In yes–no answers, *be* can occur along with the modal, but its use is optional:

Should *we be* taking a break now? Yes, we should (be). No, we shouldn't (be).

162   modals and past continuous forms

1. *Been* + a present participle follows *have* in past continuous forms with modals:

144

She *may have been kidding* when she said she was a millionaire, but I'm not sure; she *might have been telling* us the truth.

Billy, why didn't you tell me the bus was coming? You *should have been watching out for* it; now we've missed it.

In negative statements, *not* precedes *have:*

Why did Blackjack Kelly leave the casino so early? He *must not have been having* any luck.

2. Subjects follow the modal in questions:

General, *might your spies* have been giving you incorrect information about the rebels' positions? They may have been trying to double-cross (deceive) you—they might be on the rebels' side.

except when an information word is the subject:

Who should have been watering the plants while we were away?

Subjects follow *not* in negative questions:

Shouldn*'t we* have been watching the cashier more closely while he was counting out our change? I think he was short changing us.

3. In yes–no answers, a modal + (*not*) + *have* follows the subject of the answer. *Been* can also be used, but its use is optional:

Could your lawyer have been trying to double-cross you? Yes, he could have (been). No, he couldn't have (been).

Should I have been swimming in the last race, Coach? Yes, you should have (been). No, you shouldn't have (been).

Note: Contractions for a modal and *have* are not ordinarily written and are never used in formal writing; however, when dialogue is being quoted directly, as in a play or novel, the contraction *'ve* (*have*) is sometimes seen:

"Jack, you *should've* seen Babe Ruth hit the last home run of his career. It's so long ago, I can't remember when it was." (*Should've* sounds like *should-of.*)

"Timmy, you *must've* sat in some mud; the seat of your pants is all dirty." (*Must've* sounds like *must-of.*)

"Well, the dealer *might've* been bluffing when he told me he was holding the ace of spades, but I couldn't be sure." (*Might've* sounds like *might-of.*)

"We *may've* had a lot of bad luck during the last project, but it *could've* been much worse is what I keep telling myself." (*May've* sounds like *may-of,* and *could've* sounds like *could-of.*)

163 *had better;* advisability

1. Like the modal *should,* the idiom *had better* + a base form expresses advisability:

> You *had better (should)* watch out for pickpockets, muggers, and burglars when you go to the big city, young man.

> **Note:** *Had better* is quite informal and rarely appears in formal writing. Although *had better* is a past form, the idiom never refers to past time—only to the present or the future. Subject pronouns and *had* most often occur as contractions:

> Doctor, *you'd* better put on a few pounds; you're getting too thin.
> They're going shopping in the open-air market. *They'd* better watch out for pickpockets.

2. *Not* is inserted between *better* and the base form:

> You'd *better not walk* alone on these streets at night, Ma'am; there have been some muggers around the past few nights.
> Here are your keys, Sir. Your room number is 3311. Also, you and your wife had *better not keep* anything of great value in your room.

3. For emphasis, we sometimes use *just* with *had better;* it follows *had:*

> We'd *just* better not forget to lock our house when we go away on vacation; there have been a lot of burglars around in the neighborhood recently.

For added emphasis, we may insert *ever* between *not* and the base form:

> Listen, Sally, you'd just better *not ever tell* anyone this secret; if you do, I'll never speak to you again.

4. *Had better* shows a stronger sense of advisability than *should.* There is the suggestion that we might have to face an undesirable result if we do not follow the advice; it is a kind of warning:

> You'd better not ever play with matches—*you might burn yourself.*
> You'd just better keep away from those wires—*you may electrocute yourself.*
> We'd better take advantage of this opportunity—*we'll never have another chance.*

5. *Had better* is very often used in the main clause of a complex sentence followed by a subordinate clause introduced by the expression *or else* (otherwise):

> You'd better not show up late on Monday morning, Mr. Davies, *or else you'll be fired* (if you come in late).

You'd better not count on making a great deal of money on your next project, *or else you might be very disappointed* (if you don't). Don't count your chickens before they hatch. (old saying)

6. Questions do not occur with *had better* except for negative yes–no questions when we want to emphasize the advisability or warning:

> *Hadn't you* better stop teasing the monkey? He might bite you.
> *Hadn't you* better shape up, Private? You wouldn't like to be kicked out of the army, would you?

> **Pronunciation reminder:** *Hadn't you* frequently sounds like *hadn't-chew.*

7. *Had best* is occasionally heard, but it most commonly occurs in British usage:

> We'*d best* keep this information to just ourselves; we don't want it to be spread around town by the local gossips.
> Yes, we've got to plant some more bushes and little trees in the garden, but we'*d best* get rid of the snakes first.

164 *would rather;* **preference**

1. *Would rather* + a base form shows preference:

> I'*d rather be* (prefer to be) healthy than rich.
> We'*d rather live* (prefer to live) in our town than any other place in the world.

2. In statements, *than* is inserted between the two choices:

> He'd rather travel around the world *than* work in an office, but he's got no choice.
> They'd rather live in a house *than* an apartment, but they can't afford a house.

3. *Not* follows *rather* in negative verb phrases:

> I'*d rather not* stay home tonight; I'd like to go out with my friends.

In questions, we may replace *than* with *or:*

> Would you rather put off *or* call off this afternoon's meeting?
> Would you rather work for a company *or* for yourself?

However, we may use only *than* in negative questions:

> Wouldn't you rather lie down *than* sit down, Mr. Tyler? You don't look well.

Wouldn't you rather live alone *than* have to put up with that roommate of yours?

Pronunciation reminder: *Would you* sounds like *would-jew,* and *wouldn't you* sounds like *wouldn't-chew.*

Remember: *Would like* means want, but *would rather* means preference.

165   would rather have

1. *Would rather* + *have* + (*been*) + a past participle shows preference in past time:

I'd *rather have slept* on the floor last night than that terrible bed.
Would you *rather have been born* in a century other than this one?

Not follows *rather* in negative verb phrases:

I'd *rather not* have been nominated as president of our club; it's going to take a lot of my time.

2. *Would rather have* implies that the action did not take place:

I'd *rather have eaten* home last night, but my wife wanted to eat out.
We'd *rather have gotten married* when we were older, but our parents wanted us to get married right away.

166   be supposed to

1. The verb phrase *be supposed to* combined with a base form may be used in two ways:

a. *Be supposed to* can mean *it is believed that:*

Switzerland *is supposed to be* one of the most beautiful countries in the world (it is believed that Switzerland is one of the most beautiful countries in the world).

Such a statement is open to argument. For example:

Japanese trains *are supposed to be* the fastest in the world. Yes, but I believe that there are some trains in France which are even faster.
The United States *is supposed to be* one of the richest countries in the world today. Yes, but there are still a lot of poor people living here.

b. *Be supposed to* can mean *be required to* or *be expected to:*

We're *supposed to* (required to) have visas to enter Tibet.
Women *are supposed to* (expected to) wear long evening gowns at the reception at the White House this evening.

Similar in meaning to *be expected to* is *be scheduled to:*

> The Queen *is supposed to* (scheduled to) launch the new aircraft carrier this afternoon.
> Classes *are supposed to* (scheduled to) start on the hour, and not a quarter after.

Pronunciation note: *Supposed to* most often sounds like *suppose-to.*

2. *Be supposed to* is passive in construction:

> Some of the oldest people in the world *are supposed* (by people) *to* live in Georgia, a republic of the Soviet Union.

In the passive voice, *be supposed to* + *be* + a past participle often occurs:

> These passports *are supposed to be renewed* within a few months.
> These packages *are supposed to be delivered* at once.

3. When *be supposed to* is used to express a requirement, its meaning is similar to that expressed by the modal auxiliary *should:*

> People *are not supposed to* (shouldn't) litter, but they very often do.
> Class *is supposed to* (should) begin on the hour, but it sometimes doesn't.

4. The past form of *be supposed to* (meaning requirement) is also similar in meaning to the past form of *should:*

> We *were supposed to go* (should have gone) to school yesterday morning, but we decided to go to the beach instead.
> I *was supposed to renew* (should have renewed) my driver's license last month, but it completely slipped my mind (I forgot to).

5. *Be supposed to* + *be* + a present participle frequently occurs:

> Dave, we're not supposed to *be playing* our radios after midnight; it might disturb our neighbors.
> Officer, where are the police? They're supposed to *be guarding* the entrance to the Embassy; we don't want any undesirables to get in.

167   dare

1. *Dare,* which means *have the courage to,* is classified as a modal auxiliary in this textbook. Like the verb *have* (meaning possession), *dare* may occur with or without auxiliaries in questions and negatives in the simple present and past tenses:

I *dare not* say a word.   **or**   I *don't dare* say a word.
Dared he defy the King?   **or**   *Did* he *dare* defy the King?

However, as with the verb *have, dare* without auxiliaries in negatives and questions in the simple present and past tenses is chiefly British.

2. *Dare* may be followed by an infinitive with or without *to:*

Does he dare (*to*) *smoke* in a gas station?
I didn't dare (*to*) *pry* into my last roommate's private affairs.

3. When we wish to express great irritation or a certain degree of anger, we may use the pattern *how* + *dare* + subject + base form. We do not use a question mark in such sentences, as they are statements, not questions:

How dare the government (to) question my income tax form. I'm an honest taxpayer.
How dare the rich (to) treat the poor like slaves. They're just asking for trouble.

168   *need*

1. Like *dare, need* is classified as a modal auxiliary in this textbook. It may also appear with or without auxiliaries in the simple present tense:

You *needn't* work so hard.   **or**   You *don't need* to work so hard.

Need I tell more of the story?   **or**   *Do* I *need* to tell more of the story?

2. We express past time with *need have* or *did* + *need:*

I *needn't have* gone.   **or**   I *didn't need* to go.
Need he *have* done it?   **or**   *Did* he *need* to do it?

Note: *Need* without auxiliaries in negatives and questions is chiefly British.

Pronunciation note: *Need have* most frequently occurs in negative statements. *Needn't have* sounds like *needn't-of:*

You *needn't have defrosted* your refrigerator, it's automatic.

169   **perfect infinitives**

1. Infinitives have two tenses, the present (*to do, to be done, to be doing*), and the perfect (*to have done, to have been done, to have been doing*). A perfect infinitive is used to show action that took place before the action of the main verb. The verbs *appear* and *seem* most often occur in this pattern:

> Everyone in the class *appears to have fallen* asleep; I don't see one eye open.
>
> Well, Mrs. Rutherford, you no longer have that rash on your arm, I see. Yes, Doctor, it *seems to have disappeared*, thank goodness (thank God).

2. We sometimes use perfect infinitives after *would like* or *would love:*

> I'd *like to have gone* with you on your hike last weekend.
>
> Oh, I'd *love to have been* with you on your trip in Kenya; you must have had a great time.

3. Perfect infinitives occasionally follow the verb *be* combined with certain adjectives:

> We *were sorry to have missed* our train; it made us miss our boat connection in Vancouver.
>
> Mrs. Prescott, it's *nice to have met* you this afternoon. I hope we see each other again.

170 "X article" versus *the*

1a. Reminder: The pronunciation of the definite article *the* when it precedes a word that begins with a vowel sound rhymes with *tea* or *see:*

> How beautiful Acapulco is! *The air* in the evening is like magic.
>
> *The ostrich*, which is the largest bird in the world, is always burying its head in the sand.

b. "X article" (no article) occurs before a plural or uncountable noun when the noun describes some thing *in general:*

> X Water costs more than X oil in Saudi Arabia.
>
> X Apples are good for you. An apple a day keeps the doctor away. (old saying)

The, however, appears with a plural or uncountable noun when the noun describes some thing *in particular,* as in adjective phrases:

> *The water* in the bay today is almost the same color as the sky.
>
> *The apples* in this crate are all rotten (spoiled).

2. The definite article *the* is used to modify a noun that describes a particularity, but the indefinite article *a* or *an* modifies a noun that describes a generality. Compare:

> This is *a formula* for a chemical. (general, there are many chemical formulas)

CO is *the formula* for carbon monoxide. (particular, there is only *one* formula for carbon monoxide)

3. When we wish to emphasize the uniqueness of a person, place, or thing, we put a stress on *the*. Stressed *the* sounds like *the* when it precedes a noun beginning with a vowel sound:

J. W. Jaspers is *the man* you must see if you want to do business in this town. (he has all the money and power here)
Madame Cabrini is *the soprano* of the day. (no one living today has a voice as great as hers)

4. We use *the* when we are referring to a person or thing mentioned previously:

A *child* came into the room; *the child* was crying.
I saw *a kite* in the sky; *the kite* was red.

5. *The* occurs with names for objects with which we are familiar in our man-made surroundings and in our natural environment:

He walked into *the kitchen*, turned on *the light*, and opened *the refrigerator* door.
How magnificent *the mountains*, *the sky*, and *the clouds* look today!

6. The names for people of certain occupations as well as their places of business or service require *the*:

the dentist (the dentist's)   the baker (the bakery)
the butcher (the butcher's)   the watchmaker (the watchmaker's)

7. We use *the* with an adjective in the superlative degree:

Mr. Wisdom, what is *the tallest* of all existing animals?
I think San Francisco is *the most beautiful* city in the United States.

8. *The* precedes a concrete countable noun that represents a class or group (for example, a kind of animal, a kind of flower, or a kind of insect):

The fox is a very clever animal indeed.
The rose is the national flower of Spain.
The bee is always working.

Note: *A* or *an* is also used in this manner:

an elephant   a mosquito   an orchid

However, *the* emphasizes the class or group whereas *a* emphasizes an individual member of a group. *A* has the meaning of *any* in this case.

171 "X article" versus *the;* geographic names

The or "X article" occurs in many place names which refer to geography:

1. "X article" usually occurs with names of countries:

X England   X France   X Italy

Exceptions: *the* Netherlands, *the* Sudan (or X Sudan), and *the* Philippines.

2. *The* occurs with names of countries when the name refers to a political union:

the United States of America   *the* Union of Socialist Soviet Republics
the Dominican Republic   *the* Union of South Africa

3. "X article" occurs with the names of cities:

X London   X Paris   X Rome

However, *the Hague,* the capital of the Netherlands, is always preceded by *the.*
The names of a few cities retain a foreign article as part of their name:

El Paso   *Los* Angeles   *La* Paz   *Le* Havre

4. *The* accompanies the names of rivers, oceans, and seas:

the Mississippi River   *the* Atlantic Ocean   *the* Mediterranean Sea

5. "X article" occurs with the names of lakes:

X Lake Baikal   X Lake Superior   X Lake Tahoe
(but *the Lake of Lucerne, the Lake of Constance*)

However, *the* appears with the name of a group of lakes:

the Finger Lakes   *the* Great Lakes   *the* Magic Lakes

6. "X article" occurs with the names of bays:

X Biscayne Bay   X Hudson Bay   X Chesapeake Bay

But *the* may occur with the names of some bays in *of* phrases:

the Bay of Biscay   *the* Bay of Bengal   *the* Bay of Naples

7. The names of gulfs are given in *of* phrases with *the:*

the Gulf of Mexico   *the* Gulf of Thailand   *the* Gulf of Aden
(but *the* Persian Gulf)

8. "X article" occurs with the name of an island:

   X Fire Island   X Fantasy Island   X Treasure Island
   (but *the* island of Manhattan, *the* island of Bermuda, *the* island of Majorca)

The appears with the name of a group of islands:

   the Hawaiian Islands   *the* Caribbean Islands   *the* Thousand Islands

9. *The* accompanies the name of an archipelago, a desert, a forest, a canyon, or a peninsula:

   the Malay Archipelago   *the* Sahara Desert   *the* Sequoia Forest
   the Grand Canyon   *the* Iberian Peninsula

10. *The* appears with the name of a range of mountains (the word *mountains* is most often not used):

   the Andes   *the* Himalayas   *the* Alps

The name of a single mountain is usually preceded by *Mt.,* an abbreviation of *mountain;* a single mountain takes "X article":

   X Mt. Everest   X Mt. Blanc   X Mt. Kilimanjaro

   Exception: *the* Matterhorn.

11. *The* is used with points on the globe (the earth):

   the South Pole   *the* Equator   *the* Meridian

12. *The* appears with the name of a geographic area:

   the West   *the* Middle East   *the* Far East

But "X article" occurs with the name of a continent:

   X Europe   X South America   X Asia   X Africa

172 "X article" versus *the;* more place names and other uses of *the*

1. *The* is used with *university* or *college* when the name of the school follows in an *of* phrase:

   the University of Virginia   *the* College of Physicians and Surgeons

   Note: Most public (state or provincial) universities in the United States and Canada take this form.

"X article" occurs with the names of other colleges and universities:

   X Cornell University   X Mills College   X Cambridge University

2. We use *the* with libraries, museums, galleries, and archives:

> *the* Library of Congress *the* Museum of Modern Art
> *the* National Archives *the* Tate Gallery

3. *The* appears with buildings, bridges, tunnels, towers, and statues:

> *the* Empire State Building *the* Lincoln Tunnel *the* Statue of
> *the* Golden Gate Bridge *the* Eiffel Tower Liberty

4. *The* is used with the names of hotels:

> *the* Imperial Hotel *the* Grand Hotel *the* Peninsula Hotel

5. "X article" occurs with streets, avenues, boulevards, and parks:

> X Baker Street X Park Avenue X Wilshire Boulevard
> X Hyde Park

other uses of the

6. We use *the* with:

a. The names of parts of the body:

> *the* shoulders *the* arms *the* feet *the* toes

b. Official titles:

> *the* general *the* Emir *the* Maharaja *the* King

Note: Only the title and not the name is used. (Most titles are not capitalized in this case.)

c. Names of organizations:

> *the* Girl Scouts *the* United Nations *the* International Red Cross

d. Names of government agencies:

> *the* Internal Revenue Service *the* Parks Department
> *the* Department of State

e. Names of law enforcement agencies:

> *the* Federal Bureau of Investigation *the* Los Angeles Police Depart-
> (but X Scotland Yard) ment

f. Names of political parties:

> *the* Democratic Party *the* Republican Party *the* Liberal Party

Note: We often use the plural form of the political party and omit the word *party:*

> *the* Communists *the* Fascists *the* Socialists
> *the* Royalists *the* Nazis *the* Conservatives

g. Names of musical instruments:

the piano   *the* trombone   *the* tambourine   *the* xylophone

h. Names of historical periods, events, or epochs:

the Prehistoric Age   *the* Renaissance   *the* American
the Middle Ages   *the* Second World War   Revolution
                         (but X World War II)

i. Names of planets:

the planet Earth   *the* planet Mercury   *the* planet Venus
the planet Mars

"X article" occurs when we drop the word planet:

X Jupiter   X Saturn   X Uranus   X Neptune   X Pluto

Note: *The* always appears with *the sun* and *the moon*.

j. With plural names of a family when we are referring to two or more members of a family:

the Rockefellers   *the* Kennedys   *the* Rothschilds   *the* Smiths

k. Names of newspapers:

*The Chicago Tribune   The Hindustan Times   The Manchester
                                              Guardian*

7. *The* is used in time expressions with such words as:

a. *the* beginning, *the* middle, *the* end, *the* past, *the* present, *the* future

b. in *the* morning, in *the* afternoon, in *the* evening (but at X noon, at X midnight)

c. in *the* spring, in *the* summer, in *the* fall, in *the* winter; or in X spring, in X summer, etc.

8. *The* is also used in time expressions like the following:

at *the* moment   for *the* time being   during *the* year   all *the* while

9. *The* is used with the adjectives *rich* and *poor* to describe groups of people:

The rich (rich people) get richer, and *the poor* get poorer. (old saying)

173   the comparative degree of adjectives

1. A SYLLABLE is a unit of spoken language; for example, the word *few* contains one syllable; *easy* has two syllables: *eas-y; beautiful* consists of three syllables: *beau-ti-ful; intelligent* has four syllables: *in-tel-li-gent*. The syllabic division of a word may be found in any good dictionary.

2. There are three degrees for the comparison of adjectives:

    a. THE COMPARATIVE DEGREE:

    The pyramids at Cairo are *older than* the ruins of the Acropolis in Athens.

    b. THE SUPERLATIVE DEGREE:

    Mt. Everest is *the highest* mountain in the world.

    c. THE POSITIVE DEGREE:

    Our dog isn't ever *so funny as* our cat.

3. The conjunction *than* usually appears in the comparative degree:

    Two is a *more interesting* number *than* one.
    An animal free in the jungle is *happier than* one caged up in a zoo.

4. There are specific rules for forming the comparative degree:

    a. Adjectives of one syllable (except those noted in b and c below): Add *-er* to the adjective and add *than:*

    fast, *faster than*   old, *older than*   young, *younger than*

    b. Adjectives of one syllable ending in *-e*: Add *-r* to the adjective and add *than:*

    cute, *cuter than*   late, *later than*   nice, *nicer than*

    c. One-syllable adjectives ending in a final single consonant preceded by a single vowel: Double the final consonant before adding *-er* and add *than:*

    big, *bigger than*   hot, *hotter than*   thin, *thinner than*

    d. Two-syllable adjectives ending in *-y* preceded by a consonant: Change the *-y* to *-i* and add *-er* and *than:*

    easy, *easier than*   lazy, *lazier than*   crazy, *crazier than*
    funny, *funnier than*   pretty, *prettier than*   happy, *happier than*

    Exceptions: The two-syllable adjectives *friendly* and *homely* take *-er* or *more:*

    friendly, *friendlier than* (or *more friendly than*)
    homely, *homelier than* (or *more homely than*)

    e. Two-syllable adjectives ending in *-er*: Add *-er* plus *than* or use *more:*

    clever, *cleverer than* (or *more clever than*)

tender, *tenderer than* (or *more tender than*)

bitter, *bitterer than* (or *more bitter than*)

Exception: *Eager* always takes *more: more eager than.*

f. Two-syllable adjectives ending in *-ble* and *-ple*, sometimes *-tle*, *-dle:* Add *-r* plus *than* or *more . . . than:*

noble, *nobler than* (or *more noble than*)

simple, *simpler than* (or *more simple than*)

subtle, *subtler than* (or *more subtle than*)

idle, *idler than* (or *more idle than*)

g. Two-syllable adjectives ending in *-ous, -ish, -ful, -ing, -ed,* and *-less:* Place *more* before the adjective plus *than:*

famous, *more famous than*	charming, *more charming than*
foolish, *more foolish than*	relaxed, *more relaxed than*
careful, *more careful than*	careless, *more careless than*

h. Two-syllable adjectives ending in *-ct, -nt,* and *-st:* Place *more* before the adjective, and follow the adjective with *than:*

exact, *more exact than*

recent, *more recent than*

honest, *more honest than*

i. Two-syllable adjectives ending in *-ow* and *-some* can occur with either *-er* or *more:*

narrow, *narrower than* (or *more narrow than*)

shallow, *shallower than* (or *more shallow than*)

handsome, *handsomer than* (or *more handsome than*)

j. The following two-syllable adjectives may appear with either *-er* or *more:*

common	obscure	polite	quiet	secure	sincere
cruel	pleasant	profound	remote	severe	stupid

k. Adjectives of three or more syllables: Place *more* before the adjective, and follow the adjective with *than:*

enthusiastic, *more enthusiastic than*

intellectual, *more intellectual than*

l. A few adjectives are compared irregularly:

positive degree	*comparative degree*
good	better than
bad	worse than
far	$\begin{cases} \text{farther than} \\ \text{further than} \end{cases}$
little	$\begin{cases} \text{less than} \\ \text{littler than} \end{cases}$
much $\\$ many $\Big\}$	more than

Note: (a) Use *littler* when referring to size: *This is littler than that.* Use *less* when referring to amount: *I have less (time) than you do.* Rarely does *littler* occur in conversation and writing; we most often use *smaller,* the comparative degree of *small: A mouse is smaller than a rat.* (b) A traditional rule requires that *farther* be used when referring to distance: *Mercury is farther from the sun than Earth. Further* should be used to indicate additional degree: *Our company has gone further into debt.* However, today in educated informal usage, speakers often do not observe the distinction: *Our house is farther (further) than yours.*

5. *Much* is frequently used to intensify an adjective in the comparative degree:

Washington, D.C. is always *much hotter than* New York in the summertime.

Terry is *much, much handsomer than* his twin brother, Larry.

6. An adjective in its comparative degree is not always immediately followed by *than;* it is sometimes separated from *than* by a noun (+ a prepositional phrase):

Our neighbors have more *children* than we do.

She has more interesting *sentences in her paragraph* than I do in mine.

Or the adjective and *than* may be separated by an infinitive phrase:

It's more fun *to play solitaire* than it is to do nothing.

It's sometimes more dangerous *to climb down* a mountain than it is to climb up.

7. When we compare two things, persons, or conditions, an auxiliary sometimes follows the second item in the comparison, but its use is optional:

The subway is much faster than the bus (*is*).
He's got much better pronunciation than the other students (*do*).

8. When we are comparing two people, and the second item is a singular subject pronoun, we may observe either a formal or informal style:

formal: He's a better student than *I* (am).
informal: He's a better student than *me.*
formal: I'm a worse student than *he* (is).
informal: I'm a worse student than *him.*

When the second item is a plural subject pronoun, the formal style is preferred:

Our neighbors have a larger house than *we* (do); however, we have a better car than *they* (do).

174   *even* **with the comparative degree of adjectives**

The adverb *even* may be used to intensify an adjective in the comparative degree—it usually appears in an abridged clause introduced by the conjunction *but:*

My roommate's cold is very bad, but mine is *even worse.*
My hometown is far from here, but yours is *even farther.*

Note: *Than* is not used in this pattern.

175   *less* **versus** *fewer*

Less is used to modify uncountable nouns, and *fewer* is used to modify countable nouns:

He's making *less* money now because he's working *fewer* hours, but he doesn't care.
There were *fewer* women than men at the conference, but the men did *less* work.

176   *more* **versus** *less*

With adjectives of three or more syllables, the adverb *less* is often used to modify an adjective in the comparative degree:

The world now is much *less populated than* it will be in the year 2000.
In our family, the sons are *less ambitious than* the daughters.

Seldom does *less* appear with one- or two-syllable adjectives.

177 the superlative degree of adjectives

1. The definite article *the* always appears with an adjective in the superlative degree:

> *The* fastest way is not always *the* best way.
> Chile is *the* longest and *the* narrowest country in the world.

2. Rules for forming the superlative degree are as follows:

a. Adjectives of one syllable (except those noted in b and c below): Add *-est* to the adjective and *the* before the adjective:

> the highest   the oldest   the fewest   the hardest

b. Adjectives with final *-e:* Add only *-st:*

> the nicest   the wisest   the largest   the purest

c. One-syllable adjectives ending in a final single consonant preceded by a single vowel: Double the final consonant before adding *-est:*

> the biggest   the hottest   the thinnest   the grimmest

d. Two-syllable adjectives ending in *-y* preceded by a consonant: Change the *-y* to *-i* before adding *-est:*

> the easiest   the hottest   the thinnest   the fuzziest

e. Two-syllable adjectives ending in *-er:* Add *-est,* or add *the most* before the adjective:

> the cleverest (*or* the most clever)   the tenderest (*or* the most tender)
> the eagerest (*or* the most eager)

f. Two-syllable adjectives ending in *-ble* and *-ple,* sometimes *-tle, -dle:* Add *-st* or *the most:*

> the humblest (*or* the most humble)   the subtlest (*or* the most subtle)
> the simplest (*or* the most simple)   the idlest (*or* the most idle)

g. Two-syllable adjectives ending in *-ous, -ish, -ful, -ing, -ed,* and *-less:* Add *the most* before the adjective:

> the most famous   the most awful   the most developed
> the most lavish   the most liberating   the most reckless

h. Two-syllable adjectives ending in *-ct, -nt,* and *-st:* Only *the most* may appear before the adjective:

> the most exact   the most current   the most honest

i. Two-syllable adjectives ending in *-ow* and *-some* may occur with *-est* or *the most:*

the callowest (*or* the most callow)

the lonesomest (*or* the most lonesome)

j. As with the comparative degree, we may use the following two-syllable adjectives with either -*est* or *most:*

common	obscure	polite	quiet	secure	sincere
cruel	pleasant	profound	remote	severe	stupid

k. Adjectives of three or more syllables: Add *the most* before the adjective:

the most ambidextrous   the most revolutionary

the most adventuresome

l. A few adjectives are compared irregularly in the superlative degree:

positive degree	*superlative degree*
good	the best
bad	the worst
far	{ the farthest { the furthest
little	{ the least { the littlest
much } many }	the most

3. *Least* (the opposite of *most*) is sometimes used in the superlative degree, usually with adverbs of three or more syllables:

Which quiz is *the least difficult* of all the quizzes?

Ted, which is *the least expensive* to operate, your car or your wife's?

178 the comparison of equality

1. In the positive degree of adjectives, we are comparing two units (two persons, places, or things) to an equal degree:

The days are almost *as long as* the nights now; soon they'll be longer.

How fast you're growing! You're almost *as tall as* your mother now.

2. To form the positive degree of adjectives, the adverb *as* is placed before and after a given adjective. Unlike the comparative and superlative degrees of adjectives, the form of the adjective in the positive degree never changes:

(old) Love is *as old as* time. (old saying)
(young) You are *as young as* you feel. (old saying)

3. In more formal usage, when the positive degree occurs in negative comparisons, the first *as* is replaced by the adverb *so:*

Energy isn't *so* (*as*) plentiful as it was before the world started to run out of oil.
Our city isn't *so* (*as*) peaceful as it was; the times have changed.

4. Statements with adjectives in the positive degree are usually made in response to statements made by other speakers which contain false information. For example:

A: The Empire State Building in New York is the highest structure in the world.
B: I believe you're mistaken—it isn't *as high as* the Sears Tower in Chicago.
A: Money is the most important thing in the world.
B: You can't be serious—nothing is *so important as* good health.

179 the comparison of equality versus the comparative degree; *the* with adjectives and adverbs in the comparative degree

The definite article *the* sometimes occurs with adjectives and adverbs in the comparative degree in constructions like the following:

The more, the merrier.
The harder I work, *the less* I earn.
The older he gets, the wiser he becomes.
The bigger (smaller), *the better.*
The higher you climb, *the further* you have to fall.

180 certain figures of speech with *as . . . as*

Certain figures of speech with *as . . . as* occur in informal usage (rarely in formal writing). These figures of speech are sometimes considered trite and old-fashioned, but they still remain quite common in our everyday conversation. Here are just a few of the hundreds that appear in the language:

What kind of lights are you using? This room is almost *as bright as day.*
Mr. Pickwick, you're *as clever as a fox;* your ingenuity astounds me.

Why are all the shades drawn on a lovely day like this? It's *as dark as night* in this room.

Mommy, please let's eat soon—I'm *as hungry as a wolf.*

Please turn on the heat, someone; it's *as cold as ice* in here.

How glad I am I've finally graduated! I feel *as free as a bird.*

Children, when you enter the library, you should be *as quiet as a mouse.*

She says her husband is *as innocent as* a lamb (baby), but he's the one who's been doing all the stealing on the block.

When she got out of the dentist's chair, her face was *as pale as a ghost.*

We should help that old gentleman out—he's *as poor as a church mouse.*

Did I say something to embarrass you? Your face is *as red as a beet.*

Dr. Smith is a nondrinker—he's always *as sober as a judge.*

Don't be so cheap all the time, Sir; you're *as stingy as a miser.*

Look at Mr. Universe. He's *as strong as an ox* (bull).

The older he gets, the more set in his ways he becomes; he's *as stubborn as a mule.*

181   contrast and similarity; *same*

1. We may contrast two nouns with the expression *different from:*

Boys are *different from* girls.

In many ways, Americans are not *different from* Britishers.

We also use *different from* with pronouns:

How am *I* different from *you?*

Our apartment is quite different from *yours*—you're a better housekeeper.

2. *The same* + a noun + *as* is used to express a similarity:

This box is about *the same weight as* that one.

Even though this fabric is the cheapest in the store, it has *the same quality* as those that are higher priced.

3. *The same* + a noun is another way to express a similarity:

Robin takes after his father; they have *the same legs.*

My roommate and I are very different from each other; we don't want *the same things.*

4. *The same as* is also used to express a similarity:

My mother's height is exactly *the same as* mine.

A: Is Monday a better day for an appointment than Tuesday, Ma'am?
B: Monday is *the same as* Tuesday as far as I'm concerned.

182 the comparison of adverbs

1. Adverbs are compared in much the same way as adjectives. Adverbs of manner that end in *-ly* take *more than* and *the most* when they are compared:

> He doesn't speak English *as easily as* he writes it.
> He speaks it *more easily than* he can read it.
> He speaks it *the most easily* of all his classmates.
> She writes *as cleverly as* he does.
> She writes *more cleverly than* he does.
> She writes *the most cleverly* of all the students in the class.

> **Some exceptions:** The adverbs of manner *slowly, quickly,* and *loudly* may occur with -er or -est, or they can appear with *more than* or *the most:*

> Would you please drive *slower* (or *more slowly*) *than* you are; you're making me nervous.
> I don't want to speak *louder* (or *more loudly*) *than* is necessary.
> He works *the quickest* (or *the most quickly*) of all the workers in the factory.

2. With the irregular adverbs of manner like *hard* and *fast,* we do not use *more* or *most*—we add only *-er* or *-est:*

> He works *as hard as* anyone else in the office.
> He works *harder than* any of the others.
> He works *the hardest* of all.
> She throws *as fast as* anyone else on her team.
> She throws *faster than* all the other players.
> Of everyone on the team, she throws *the fastest.*

3. Adverbs of time like *early, late,* and *soon* also take *-er* or *-est:*

> earlier than, the earliest   later than, the latest
> sooner than, the soonest

4. *Less . . . than* and *the least* are sometimes used in the comparison of adverbs (usually with adverbs of three or more syllables):

> She operates *less efficiently than* the other managers.
> He operates *the least efficiently* of all the operators in this plant.

5. *Less than* frequently follows many verbs:

He cooks *less than* I do.
Male lions hunt *less than* the females do.
I jog *less than* my roommate does.

6. A few adverbs are compared irregularly:

positive degree	*comparative degree*	*superlative degree*
well	better than	the best
badly	worse than	the worst
far	farther (further than)	the farthest (furthest)
much	more than	the most
little	less than	the least

183 gerunds and gerund phrases as subjects

1. An *-ing* form of a verb is called a GERUND when it is used in the same manner as a noun. Like nouns, gerunds may be used as the subject of a sentence:

Running regularly will make you feel better, Doctor.
Studying requires most of my time during the day.

2. An *-ing* form is called a PRESENT PARTICIPLE when it is used as a verb:

His watch hasn't been *running* for more than a year, but he's still wearing it.
The son of some friends of mine is *studying* to be a Catholic priest.

3. A gerund combined with a prepositional phrase is called a GERUND PHRASE:

Running in the Olympics for a gold medal is our daughter's life ambition.
Studying at the library is fun; that's where I see all my friends.

4. Occasionally, most often in formal writing and speaking, possessive adjectives and nouns precede the gerund in a gerund phrase:

Her listening in on her boss's conversations caused her to lose her job.
The dog's barking woke up everyone in the neighborhood last night.

5. Gerund phrases may be in the passive voice; the gerund *being* is the auxiliary in a passive gerund phrase:

Being asked by the Professor to leave the room was embarrassing for me.

Being escorted to the dance by a handsome movie star was a thrill for her.

6. A gerund phrase may also contain the idiom *have to* as a gerund:

Having to go to school on Sunday morning is not very pleasant, is it?
Having to do homework is good for the students. They learn faster.

184 gerunds as objects of certain verbs

1. There are some verbs that cannot be followed by an infinitive. Compare:

correct	incorrect
I enjoy *studying*.	I enjoy [to study].
Would you mind *being* quiet?	Would you mind [to be] quiet?

Some verbs that must be followed by a gerund are:

admit	deny	finish	miss	quit	risk
avoid	detest	give up	postpone	recall	stop
consider	dislike	keep on	practice	recommend	(= quit)
delay	enjoy	mind	put off	resist	suggest
					tolerate

2. An infinitive follows the verb *stop* if we mean *to stop for a purpose:*

I *stopped to buy* the morning paper on my way to work.
While I was walking in the park, I *stopped to watch* some children flying kites.

When *stop* means *to quit,* however, a gerund must follow it.

The machine was working perfectly when it suddenly *stopped running.*
He *stopped sending* Christmas cards a few years ago, so he receives almost none.

3. In idiomatic usage, a gerund follows the verb phrase *can't help:*

I *can't help feeling* sorry for that poor and lonely old woman.
She *can't help loving* that wonderful man.

4. Certain gerunds follow the verb *go* in idiomatic usage:

Let's go *bowling* tonight, everyone; it'll be a lot of fun.
Listen, Beverly, would you like to go *dancing?* It's Saturday night.
We should have gone *shopping* for food; the refrigerator is completely empty.

When I was a boy, I used to go *fishing* almost every day during the summer.

Do you ever go *jogging* in the park? It's a good way to keep in shape.

While we were in London, we went *hunting* for antiques all the time.

During our vacation in Bali, we would go *swimming* three or four times a day.

Let's go *skating*—I'll race you to Central Park.

When we were in Paris, we only went *window-shopping*. We couldn't afford to buy anything.

We went *skin diving* a lot while we were in Cozumel—it's on the Caribbean.

It's been snowing for a week in the mountains now. Let's go *skiing*.

Last summer in Nepal, we'd usually go *hiking* somewhere every morning.

The wind isn't blowing much, so we're not going *sailing* this afternoon.

I never went *mountain-climbing* when I was in Switzerland—I was afraid to.

185   gerund versus infinitive

There are certain verbs that can be followed by a gerund or an infinitive; there is no difference in meaning. Compare:

gerund	*infinitive*
I *like dancing* the cha cha cha.	I *like to dance* the cha cha cha.
I *hesitate telling* you this news.	I *hesitate to tell* you this news.

Some verbs that may be followed by a gerund or an infinitive are:

attempt	continue	intend	plan
begin	dread	like	prefer
cannot bear (= tolerate)	hate	love	start
cannot stand (= tolerate)	hesitate	neglect	try

186   gerunds and gerund phrases as objects of prepositions

1. Because they may function as nouns, gerunds and gerund phrases can also occur as objects of prepositions. Two usual patterns are:

a. verb + preposition + gerund (phrase):

He *believes in praying*. He *believes in praying to many different gods;* he's a Hindu.

b. adjective + preposition + gerund (phrase):

Most people are *afraid of falling*. Many people are *afraid of falling in love*.

2. An object may separate a verb from a preposition:

Thank you for helping me out so much during the last project.
Bad weather *prevented us from* going on the hike that we'd planned.

187 gerunds and gerund phrases as objects of prepositions; negative gerund phrases

The adverb *not* precedes the gerund in a negative gerund phrase:

Not being acquainted with the neighborhood late at night, Mr. Brown became frightened and started to run.
I'll enjoy *not having* to work today; it'll give me a chance to rest up.
Thank you, Mrs. Griffith, for *not telling* my wife about the surprise I'm planning for her.

188 gerunds in time phrases

Gerunds are often used in time phrases:

Please wash your hands *before leaving the room.*
Since becoming a father for the first time, Howard has become a new man.

You will remember that a phrase never has a subject or a verb but a clause always does. Compare:

time phrase	**time clause**
When shopping for clothes, he always takes his wife along.	*When he shops for clothes,* he always takes his wife along.
Until coming to the Sahara, she'd never seen a camel before.	*Until she came to the Sahara,* she'd never seen a camel before.

189 *worth, rather than,* and *instead of*

Gerunds must follow the adjective *worth* and the expressions *rather than* and *instead of*:

This old carpet isn't worth anything—it isn't even *worth giving away.*
Instead of eating home tonight, let's go out for Chinese food.

Would you rather go to Asia or Europe this summer? *Rather than going anywhere,* why don't we just stay home?

Note: *No use, no good,* and *no need* combined with expletives (*it* or *there*) may be followed by a gerund or an infinitive:

It's *no use complaining* (or *to complain*) to the government authorities; they'll do nothing about the situation.
It's *no good crying* (or *to cry*) over your past mistakes; there's nothing you can do about them now.
There's *no need worrying* (or *to worry*) about anything; everything will be taken care of for you, Ma'am.

190   *be used to* and *get used to*

1. *Be used to* means *be accustomed to:*

I'm not *used to* (accustomed to) the customs of this country; I've just gotten here.
Sir, I'm not *used to* (accustomed to) being treated like an inferior; you must treat me with respect.

2. *Get used to* means *become accustomed to:*

Are you finally *getting used to* (becoming accustomed to) being a student in this school?
While living in India, I could never *get used to* (become accustomed to) eating rice with my fingers.

191   *used to* + a base form

1. *Used to* + a base form is used for a condition which once existed but which no longer does:

Istanbul *used to be called* Constantinople.
Tokyo *used to be* the largest city in the world (I believe Shanghai is now the largest).

2. Sometimes, *used to* is used for a condition that existed in past time and still does:

Ho Chi Minh City *used to be called* Saigon, and it still is by many people.
I *used to ride* a bicycle a lot when I was a child, and I still do.

3. *Used to* is most frequently used for expressing a past custom (or habitual activity) that occurred with regularity in past time but now no longer does:

> When I was a child on a farm in California many years ago, I *used to go* out in the fields early every morning to get the cows for my father to milk. When I got home from school in the afternoons, I *used to feed* the ducks and chickens, pick vegetables for dinner, and build a fire for the evening. I *used to do* these chores every day.

4. *Anymore* and *any longer* are frequently found in negative clauses in sentences containing *used to*:

> He *used to bring* flowers to his wife all the time, but he doesn't *anymore*.
> She *used to be* an honest person, but she isn't *any longer;* money has corrupted her.

5. Negative statements with *used to* (in the base form) are not so common with past custom, but they occur in sentences such as the following:

> I *didn't use to have* much appreciation for Indian music, but now I do.
> We *didn't use to have to pay* a lot for electricity, but now we do.

6. As in negative statements, *used to* becomes a base form in questions:

> Did you *use* to enjoy playing house when you were a child?
> Mr. Perkins, what kind of work did you *use* to do before you dropped out of society and became a hippie?

However, the idiom does not change in form when the information word is the subject:

> That strange old house looks haunted. *Who used to live* in it?
> *Who used to run* this office before you took over the job?

> **Pronunciation note:** *Used* (before *to*) sounds like *use* (pronounced as a noun).

192 -ing forms following sense perception verbs

1. A base form or an *-ing* form may occur as the object of certain sense perception verbs. Some of the sense perception verbs are:

> feel   hear   notice   observe   see   smell   watch

The noun or pronoun between the verb and the *-ing* form is called the subject of the *-ing* form; it is also the "doer," the agent that performs the action.

Have you ever *seen bees* (subject) *collecting* (or *collect*) nectar for making honey?

In biology lab yesterday, we observed a *spider* (subject) *spinning* (or *spin*) a web.

2. An -*ing* form after sense perception verbs emphasizes the *duration* of an event, whereas a base form after such verbs suggest the action *was completed.* Compare:

Daddy, have you ever watched a calf *being born?* Does it take a long time?

When Bessie, my cow, was having her calf, my neighbor was there to help me—he'd already seen several calves *be born,* so he knew what to do.

Note: An infinitive never occurs in this pattern. Compare:

correct	*incorrect*
I saw some kittens being born.	I saw some kittens [to be born].
We watched an elephant eat his dinner.	We watched an elephant [to eat] his dinner.

193 -*ing* versus -*ed* adjectives

1. An -*ing* or -*ed* participle may occur as an adjective:

What a *charming* woman your wife is, Mr. Hawkins!

I'm *charmed* by your beautiful and well-behaved children, Ma'am.

How *tiring* this job is! I'm working like a slave.

He's *tired,* but he's still going to play another nine holes of golf.

2. An -*ing* adjective usually occurs with things, and an -*ed* adjective most often appears with nouns or pronouns designating people. Compare:

The movie is *boring.* I am *bored* with the movie.

Are these results *satisfying,* Gentlemen? Yes, we're quite *satisfied.*

The bad weather is disappointing. Everyone is *disappointed* with the bad weather.

However, occasionally -*ing* adjectives appear with people:

He is a *boring* actor (he bores audiences). He is a *bored* actor (he is bored with life—everything bores him).

She is an *interesting* writer (many readers are *interested* in what she has to say). She is *interested* in writing an article about the life of a bee (that should be *interesting*).

3. The verb *develop* is frequently used as an *-ing* or *-ed* adjective. *Developed* means something is already developed:

> Japan is the most *developed* country in Asia.

Developing means something is still in the process of being developed:

> Nepal is one of the poorest *developing* countries in the world; it is also one of the most beautiful.

194   make, let, and *help*

1. The verbs *make* (meaning *compel* or *force*) and *let* (meaning *allow* or *permit*) are always followed by a noun or pronoun plus a base form. We may refer to the noun or pronoun in such a pattern as the "doer," the agent that performs the action:

> My dog didn't want to go for a swim in the river, but I *made him jump* in (I just gave him a little push).
> Why did the teacher *make Dickie stay* after class yesterday afternoon?
> Why do they *let their child* do anything he wants? They'll spoil him.
> Don't *let the cat get* to the food on the table. Watch him.

Note: Never use an infinitive after *make* or *let*. Compare:

correct	*incorrect*
Don't make me make a mistake.	Don't make me [to make] a mistake.
Don't let the kitten scratch you.	Don't let the kitten [to scratch] you.

2. The verb *help* may be followed by a base form or an infinitive. Like *make* and *let, help* is always followed by a "doer":

> Doctor, please help me *get* (or *to get*) well; I want to be my old self again.
> He'd like to help his wife *clean* (or *to clean*) the house, but she doesn't want him to.

In some cases, however, the "doer" is understood:

> Her husband doesn't want to help (her) take care of the children.
> Edith, would you like me to help (you) do the puzzle?

195   **perfect participial phrases**

1. A PARTICIPIAL PHRASE is a modifying phrase consisting of a participle and its objects (or complements) and modifiers:

> *Wringing her hands nervously,* Maria waited for the long-distance call. (Modifies the noun *Maria.*)

The material *delivered on May 15* was seriously damaged. (Modifies the noun *material*.)

2. In rather formal usage, perfect participial phrases in the active voice occur:

Having read the article in the paper (because I *have read* the article), I have a much better understanding of the situation now.

Having finished a project (after he *has finished* a project), he never wants to go back to it.

Having seen the movie (because I *had seen* the movie), I didn't want to see it again.

Having done all his chores (after he *had done* all his chores), he was ready to do his homework.

3. The adverbs *not* and *never* precede the auxiliary in negative phrases:

Not having had much education, the poor woman wasn't able to find a good job.

Never having been in love before, the young man didn't understand the sensation he was feeling.

196 *so, such, such a,* and *such an;* adverbial *that* clauses

1. A RESULT CLAUSE is a type of adverbial clause; it is used to show the result of another clause:

His feet are so big (situation) *that it's difficult for him to find shoes* (result).

2. The subordinate conjunction *so that* is used in a sentence containing a result clause; however, it is "split" in a variety of ways:

a. Split by adjective (+ prepositional phrase):

He is *so* angry (at his sister) *that* he won't speak to her.

The poor woman was *so* unhappy (with her situation) *that* she drowned herself.

b. Split by adjective + noun (+ prepositional phrase):

There are *so* many mistakes (in this composition) *that* you must do it over.

There are *so* few people (in the audience) *that* the theater might cancel the performance. If it does, I want my money back.

Note: The adjectives *much, many, little,* and *few* often occur in this pattern.

c. Split by adverb (+ prepositional phrase):

He worked *so* hard (at the office today) *that* he's completely worn out this evening.

She was singing *so* beautifully (at the concert) *that* my eyes filled with tears.

3. In informal usage, *that* is omitted and replaced by a comma in writing and a pause in speech:

She's so beautiful, (pause) I can't believe my eyes.

That story is so terrible, (pause) I won't ever be able to believe it.

4. *Such that* is also used in complex sentences containing result clauses:

They have such a big house (situation) *that their guests are always getting lost* (result).

5. Like *so that, such that* is "split" in a variety of ways:

a. Split by *a (an)* + adjective + singular countable noun (+ prepositional phrase):

I saw *such* a funny cartoon (in the magazine) *that* I couldn't stop laughing.

I'd had *such* an inspiring conversation (with the prophet) *that* I wanted to go speak to him again.

b. Split by adjective + plural countable noun (+ prepositional phrase):

He's saying *such* foolish things (to people) *that* everyone is laughing at him.

She's having *such* terrible nightmares (during her naps) *that* she's planning to go to a psychiatrist.

c. Split by adjective + uncountable noun (+ prepositional phrase):

We had *such* wonderful weather (during our vacation) *that* we spent most of our time in the outdoors.

He's doing *such* top-secret research (for the government) *that* he can't talk about it to anyone, not even his wife.

6. In informal usage, *that* is omitted and replaced by a comma in writing and a pause in speech:

He is such a handsome man, (pause) everyone thinks he's a movie
star.

It's such a cold day, (pause) I don't want to take even one step outside.

197 clauses of purpose with *so that*

1. *So that* is also used to introduce a PURPOSE CLAUSE. Like a clause of
reason introduced by *because,* a purpose clause may answer a *why* question:

> (*Why* did you go to the bakery?) I went to the bakery *so that I could
> buy a birthday cake.*
> (*Why* are you going to the beach?) We're going to the beach *so that we
> can go for a swim.*

2. In informal usage, particularly in speaking, *that* is omitted:

> We'd like to go to Egypt so we can see the pyramids and visit Luxor.
> They wanted to go to Arizona so they could see the Grand Canyon.

Punctuation note: No comma, with or without *that,* is used in this
pattern.

3. Most often, the modals *may, can,* and *will* (and their past forms) are
the verb forms used in purpose clauses introduced by *so that:*

> We'd like to go to Washington, D.C. in April so that *we may* see the
> cherry trees blossoming.
> Those people are on their way to Nepal so they *can* climb Mt. Everest.
> They're taking a train from Bangkok to Singapore so that their trip *will*
> cost less, and they will see more.
> We wanted to stop in Agra on our way to Bombay so we *might* see the
> Taj Mahal.
> When they went to Germany, they rented a yacht so that they *could* go
> cruising on the Rhine.
> I got to the airport in Rome two hours early so I *wouldn't* miss my flight
> to Athens, but the flight had been cancelled.

Note: When *that* is omitted, it is sometimes difficult to tell whether
so is a coordinate conjunction, as in:

> Nothing much was happening at the meeting, *so* we decided to leave
> early. (result)

or whether it is a subordinate conjunction:

> We decided to leave early *so* we wouldn't get home late. (purpose)

A good rule to follow is: When *so* cannot be used with *that,* it is a
coordinate conjunction like *and* and *but.* For example, in *I was hun-*

gry, so I ate two hamburgers, so is a coordinate conjunction and the sentence is compound, not complex—we cannot use *that*. Also note that we use a comma in this case.

198 *in order* + **an infinitive**

1. *In order* + an infinitive phrase is also used to show purpose:

I've got to go to the drugstore *in order to get* a prescription (so that I can get a prescription).

I'd like to go to the stationery store *in order to look for* a birthday card for my dad (so that I may look for a birthday card for my dad).

2. *In order* can be omitted and an infinitive phrase itself can show purpose:

It's a large tree; I've got to use a big axe (in order) *to cut it down*.

I've got to stop at 65th Street (in order) *to drop these packages off*.

3. An infinitive phrase with *in order* may appear in initial position followed by a comma:

(*In order*) *To catch up with the rest of the class*, you must study hard.

(*In order*) *To speak and write English well*, you must take another course.

4. *Not* follows *in order* in negative verb phrases:

In order not to get lost, I suggest you take along a good map of the park.

You'd better keep your watch on your wrist *in order not* to lose it.

5. The preposition *for* + a noun may be used to show purpose in a prepositional phrase:

We want to climb to the top of the mountain *for a good view* of the valley.

We're going to Rio de Janeiro this year *for Carnival*.

Note: Do not confuse a *for* phrase with an infinitive phrase:

I went to the bakery for (not *for to buy*) some bread.

We went to the gym for (not *for to get*) some exercise.

6. *What . . . for* is a separable colloquial expression meaning *why*. It is used informally to ask information questions that require an answer either with a *for* phrase or with *in order* plus an infinitive phrase:

What did you go to the bank *for?* . . . (for) some money. . . . (in order) to get some money.

What do you need a visa *for?* . . . (for) a trip to China. . . . (in order) to take a trip to China.

199 *despite* and *in spite of*

1. You will recall that we use the subordinate conjunctions *though, even though,* and *although* to introduce adverbial clauses of concession to complex sentences:

> The revolutionary forces hanged the general *even though he had always been on their side.*
>
> *Although everyone knows the truth about the government scandal,* no one wants to talk about it.

2. The concessive prepositions *despite* and *in spite of* may be combined with a noun:

> *Despite the heat* (even though it's hot), I'm going to go sightseeing. I want to see Baghdad.
>
> *In spite of the cold* (even though it's cold), I'm going to take a walk. I want to see what Moscow is like.

3. *Despite* and *in spite of* combined with *the fact* (*that*) may be used as subordinate conjunctions to introduce clauses of concession:

> *Despite the fact* (*that*) he's never been to school, he reads and writes well.
>
> *In spite of the fact* (*that*) he lives alone, he's never lonely.

200 adverbial *that* clauses after adjectives of feeling and emotion

1. An adverbial clause introduced by the subordinate conjunction *that* may follow a main clause which contains a form of the verb *be* and an adjective expressing feeling or emotion.

> The people of the nation were shocked *that the high government official had been assassinated.*
>
> I'm sorry *that I didn't study English more when I was younger.*

2. A *that* clause after adjectives expressing feeling and emotion can be similar in meaning to a clause introduced by *because:*

We are proud that (because) all our children have done well in their careers.

The people of the world were astonished that (because) a man had been able to land on the moon.

3. Adverbial *that* clauses tell *why:*

(*Why* are you so furious?) I'm furious *that someone has picked my pocket.*

(*Why* is he so jealous?) He's jealous *that his wife has a better job than he does.*

4. We use *that* clauses after main clauses that contain the following adjectives (a partial list):

afraid	confident	envious	glad	jealous	sad
angry	conscious	fearful	(un)happy	positive	sorry
(un)certain	content	furious	hopeful	proud	sure

5. Adverbial *that* clauses also follow main clauses that contain the following -*ed* participial adjectives (a partial list):

amazed	contented	impressed	satisfied	thrilled
annoyed	depressed	irritated	shocked	troubled
ashamed	disappointed	perplexed	startled	worried
astonished	disgusted	pleased	stunned	
concerned	excited	relieved	surprised	

6. In informal usage, *that* may be omitted:

News dispatches say the government is confident (that) the rebel forces have been put down.

They are sad (that) their daughter and son-in-law are moving away.

However, *that* is not ordinarily omitted when the adverbial clause follows an -*ed* participial adjective.

The professor is pleased *that* the class has made so much progress since the beginning of the semester.

My grandfather is satisfied *that* he has led a long, happy, and prosperous life.

201 future-possible real conditions; the simple present tense and its continuous form in *if* clauses

1. A FUTURE–POSSIBLE CONDITIONAL STATEMENT consists of a conditional (subordinate) clause introduced by the subordinate conjunction *if* and a result (main) clause. Usually, the verb in the *if* clause is in the simple present tense or its continuous form. The verb in the result clause is most often in the future tense:

> If you *don't do* your homework this coming semester (condition), you *won't make* much progress (result).
>
> If it's *raining* tomorrow (condition), *we'll still go* on our picnic (result).

Memorize: The simple present tense and its continuous form after *if* may express an event in future time.

2. A conditional (*if*) clause may occur in initial or final position:

> *If you don't brush your teeth,* you'll get cavities.
> You'll get cavities *if you don't brush your teeth.*

Punctuation reminder: When a subordinate adverbial clause occurs in initial position, a comma usually follows:

> *If the rich do not do more for the poor,* there will be a revolution.

3. In addition to being in the future tense, the result clause can be in the present continuous tense:

> If I have enough money, I'm *sending* flowers to my mother on her birthday.

or in the imperative mood:

> If you do go to Yugoslavia in September, *go* to Dubrovnik.

or contain *be going to* + a base form:

> You're *going to lose* money if you don't change your business methods.

202 the present perfect tense in *if* clauses

The present perfect tense sometimes appears in *if* clauses in order to emphasize the fact that an event has been completed before the event in the result clause. Almost always, adverbial expressions of time like *by the end of the day* and *within three weeks* occur in such sentences:

> If the patient *hasn't started* to feel better *by the end of the week,* the doctor will probably prescribe another series of treatments.
>
> You won't have to pay income taxes if you *have made* less than a thousand dollars *by the end of the year.*

203 *should* in conditional clauses

1. The modal *should* means *happen to* when it occurs in *if* clauses:

> If I *should* (happen to) get homesick during my vacation, I'll come home right away.
> We'll just go to bed earlier than usual if the lights *should* (happen to) go out.

2. We may drop the *if* and put *should* before the subject as in a question form:

> *Should we* lose our way, we'll find it again; we've got a good map and compass.

Expletive *there* frequently appears in such sentences:

> *Should there* be a telegram for you, I will let you know at once.

3. Result clauses containing verbs in the imperative mood often accompany conditional clauses with *should:*

> Should there be a fire, *walk, don't run, to the nearest exit.*
> Should you run out of money, *don't hesitate to ask me for a loan.*

4. *Not* follows the subject in negative verb phrases:

> Should I *not* be here when you get back, please do wait for me.

204 *can, must,* and *have to* in *if* clauses; *had better*

1. The modal *can* frequently occurs in *if* clauses:

> If our car *can* be fixed by tomorrow, we'll really appreciate it.
> I'll give you a thousand dollars if you *can* keep your head under water for four minutes.

2. *Must* makes a less frequent appearance than *can* in *if* clauses, but when it does, the verb in the result clause is usually in the imperative mood:

> If you *must* turn on the radio, *please don't turn it up too loud.*
> Children, if you *must* sit on the floor, *please sit on the rug.*

3. The idioms *have to* (*have got to*) and *be able to* often appear in *if* clauses:

> If this letter *has to* be done over, I'm going to complain to my boss.
> If it's *got to* be done over, she can do it herself.

If you're *not able to* make it to the meeting, I'll be glad to relay any messages for you.

4. We may use the above idioms in both *if* and result clauses. However, the idiom *had better* may occur only in result clauses:

You'd *better* do your homework now if you don't want to do it tomorrow morning.
If that sore on your arm doesn't heal up within a few days, you'd *better* go to the clinic.

205 *will* in *if* clauses

When *will* appears in an *if* clause, we are making a very polite and formal request:

If you *will* please sit down, Sir, your request will be attended to.
If you *will* excuse me for a few minutes, I've got to make a phone call.

Note: *Would* also appears in this kind of polite request:

If you *would* please sit down, Ma'am, you would be more comfortable.

206 *unless, even if,* and *in case*

1. *Unless* means *if not.* It may replace *if* to introduce clauses in future-possible conditions:

We won't lay down our arms *unless our enemy lays down theirs* (if our enemy doesn't lay down theirs).

2. Although verbal phrases in *unless* clauses have the same form as those in *if* clauses, a negative verb phrase usually expresses an affirmative condition, and an affirmative verb phrase usually expresses a negative condition:

We'll go skiing tomorrow *unless it doesn't snow* (if it snows) tonight.
We won't go skiing tomorrow *unless it snows* (if it doesn't snow) tonight.

3. *Unless* almost always introduces conditional clauses containing affirmative verb phrases. The result clause in the same sentence usually contains a negative verb phrase but not always:

We won't be able to buy a house unless the bank *lends* us some money.

Unless someone *invents* a reasonably priced substitute for oil, the world is going to be heading for an *extremely serious* shortage of energy.

4. We may emphasize a condition with *even if:*

Even if the poor man works ten hours a day, he'll never be able to save any money.
My partner and I will reach the top of this mountain *even if* it means we must risk our lives to do it.

5. *In case* is most often used in sentences where instructions are being given in the result clause:

In case you run out of money (or lose it) while traveling, *you should wire me immediately.*
Please go to the drugstore immediately in case you run out of your medicine.

207 questions with conditional clauses

Like all other adverbial clauses, conditional clauses do not change in form in yes–no and information questions:

If you have time tomorrow, will you help me move to my new apartment?
Will you want to go out this *evening even if it's raining?*
What will you wear to the palace *if you are invited?*

208 real conditions; *if* meaning *when*

REAL CONDITIONS are used to show a generalization about events that sometimes take place in present time with some kind of regularity. When this occurs, *if* has the meaning of *when* or *whenever* (it does not mean a condition), and the simple present tense or its continuous form indicates present time (not future time) in both the *if* and result clauses:

If (when, whenever) our children are doing their homework, my husband and I always try to be quiet.
If (when, whenever) we spend money foolishly, we usually regret it later.

209 present-unreal conditions

1. A PRESENT–UNREAL CONDITIONAL STATEMENT consists of a conditional clause introduced by the subordinate conjunction *if* and a result clause. A past form is most often used in the *if* clause to mean present time, and *would* plus a base form occurs in the result clause:

> If I *had* a lot of money in the bank right now, I *would invest* it in real estate.
>
> I *wouldn't be* in this class if I *spoke* English well.

Memorize: A verb in the simple past tense after *if* in present-unreal conditions means present time.

Note: The use of *should* in the first person is chiefly British:

> If I wanted to buy a nice woolen suit, I *should* go to London to shop for it.
>
> We *should* be disappointed if we didn't have our usual afternoon tea.

2. A present-unreal conditional (if) clause expresses a situation that is contrary to reality—in other words, unreal. Compare:

reality	*condition*
I don't have a million dollars.	*If I had a million dollars,* I'd never have to work again.
He doesn't love her.	*If he really loved her,* he wouldn't treat her like a slave.

3. The result clause in a present-unreal conditional statement shows a hypothetical result. It draws a conclusion based on the condition expressed in the conditional clause. Compare:

condition	*hypothetical result*
If I didn't have any money,	I'd borrow some from a classmate.
If I had his phone number,	I'd call him up now.

4. Besides *would,* the modals *could* and *might* and the idioms *be able to* and *have to* may occur in result clauses:

> I *could* make myself invisible if I knew how to work miracles.
>
> If I had a $150,000 right now, I *might* build a house, but I'm not sure.
>
> If you spoke English well, you'd *be able to* find a good job right away.
>
> We wouldn't *have to* worry about a thing if we had more money.

Punctuation reminder: When a subordinate adverbial clause appears in initial position, a comma usually follows:

> A: Mr. Smith, *if you knew what the President knows,* you wouldn't be able to sleep at night.
>
> B: Sir, I don't know what the President knows, and I'm still not able to sleep at night.

5. The verb *be* has a special (subjunctive) form in a present-unreal conditional clause; *were* is used in all persons:

> If I *were* the president of this country, I'd do things very differently.

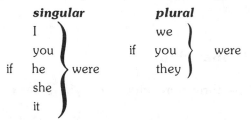

	singular			**plural**	
	I			we	
	you		if	you	were
if	he	were		they	
	she				
	it				

Memorize: *Were* follows *if* in all persons in present-unreal conditions.

Note: *Was* is sometimes seen, most often heard, in such clauses. Its use is nonstandard, however, and it does not appear in educated speech and writing.

210   continuous forms in *if* clauses

Continuous forms may occur in both the *if* and result clauses in the present-unreal:

> If he *were making* more money, he *wouldn't be complaining* about his job.
> I *wouldn't be lying* here in bed if I *weren't feeling* so tired.

211   *unless* and *even if*

1. Reminder: *Unless* means *if not:*

> He wouldn't be marrying her unless he *loved* her (*if* he *didn't love* her).
> You wouldn't be able to find a job in Paris easily unless you *spoke* French well (*if* you *didn't speak* French well).

2. Reminder: We may emphasize a condition with *even if:*

> *Even if* I were very poor, I'd still be the happiest man in town; I've got a wonderful wife.
> Grace never likes anything; she's always complaining. She wouldn't be satisfied *even if* she were living in a palace.

3. The idioms *have to* and *be able to* often occur in present-unreal conditions:

If I didn't *have to* work in order to make a living, I would spend all my time on my personal projects and hobbies—it would be wonderful.

I could become one of the richest persons in the world if I *were able to* predict events in the future.

212   *could* in conditional clauses

The modal *could* + a base form sometimes occurs in *if* clauses to express ability or possibility:

If I *could* do everything as well as you can, I'd be a much happier person.

Someone I know would give me a thousand dollars if I *could* keep my head under water for four minutes. I'm afraid I can't do it.

Note: A common response to a question like *Can you help/tell/show me?* is:

No, I'm sorry, I would if I could, but I can't.

213   questions with conditional clauses

1. Reminder: Like all other adverbial clauses, conditional clauses do not change in form in yes–no and information questions:

If you suddenly were a millionaire, would you keep on working at your present job?

What would you do first *if you were suddenly a millionaire?*

2. In conversation, we frequently omit the *if* clause in a conditional statement when that clause is understood:

Would your life change much (*if you were suddenly a millionaire*)?

(*If you were suddenly a millionaire*), you wouldn't forget your friends, would you?

3. Also in conversation, we occasionally use the conditional clause *if I were you* or *if you were I* (*they, she,* etc.). A formal or informal style may be observed:

formal: If you were I, Your Majesty, would you want to have higher taxes?

informal: If you were me, Sam, how would you deal with my landlord?

formal: If I were he, I wouldn't criticize the school so much.

informal: If I were him, I'd try to play better this season; he might get kicked off the team if he doesn't.

formal: If I were they, I wouldn't spend all my money having a good time; they should start thinking about the future.
informal: If I were them, I wouldn't be goofing off all the time; they'd better settle down, or else they might get kicked out of school.

214 past-unreal conditions

1. A PAST-UNREAL CONDITIONAL STATEMENT usually consists of an *if* clause that contains a verb in the past perfect tense, and a result clause containing *would have* (+ been) + a past participle:

> If there *had been* more time yesterday, another quiz *would have been given.*
> I *wouldn't have eaten* the forbidden fruit if I *had been* Adam or Eve.

Pronunciation note: *Would have* sounds like *would-of,* and *wouldn't have* sounds like *wouldn't-of.*

Reminder: *'d* followed by a past participle (*'d done*) is a contraction of *had; 'd* followed by a base form (*'d do*) is a contraction of *would.*

2. A past-unreal conditional clause expresses a situation in past time that was contrary to fact or reality—in other words, unreal. Compare:

reality	*condition*
I wasn't Romeo.	*If I had been Romeo,* I wouldn't have killed myself.
My alarm clock rang this morning.	*If it hadn't rung,* I would have been late to class.

3. Result clauses in past conditional statements show a hypothetical conclusion based on the condition expressed in the conditional clause. Compare:

condition	*result*
If Romeo hadn't killed himself,	he and Juliet would have been reunited.
If Adam and Eve hadn't eaten the forbidden fruit,	they would have been able to stay in Paradise.

215 continuous forms in *if* clauses

Continuous forms may occur in both conditional and result clauses:

> If you'd *been using* your dictionary while you were writing your composition, you wouldn't have made so many spelling errors.

If your grandfather had saved more money when he was younger, he *wouldn't have been working* so hard almost up to the time of his death.

216   unless and even if; could have in result clauses

1. Reminder: *Unless* means *if not:*

> He wouldn't have enjoyed the movie unless his wife *had gone* with him (if his wife *hadn't gone* with him).
> I wouldn't have gone into the city yesterday unless I *had had* an important appointment (if I *hadn't had* an important appointment).

2. Reminder: We may emphasize a condition with *even if:*

> *Even if* I had suddenly become a millionaire, I would never have quit my job.
> He wouldn't have gone into the army *even if* he'd been drafted—it's against his religious beliefs.

3. We use *could have* (+ been) + a past participle in a result clause to express:

a. Ability:

> If the piano hadn't been so heavy, it *could have been pushed* into the other room.

b. Possibility:

> He *could have become* a great man if he hadn't been such a playboy.

c. Impossibility:

> Impossible! That woman *couldn't have robbed* the bank even if there had been no police around; she's almost 90 years old.

217   could have and might have in result clauses

We also use *might have* (+ been) + a past participle in result clauses to show conjecture or possibility:

> If you'd studied harder, you *might not have done* so badly on the exam.
> That man *might have been elected* the president if he had had the support of the people.

218   could have in conditional clauses

Could have (+ been) + a past participle occasionally occurs in past-unreal conditions (*if* clauses). *Could have* following *if* means *had been able to; could not have* means *had not been able to:*

> If I *could have had* (had been able to have) a bit more time, I would have been able to finish the exam.
> We would have been disappointed if we *couldn't have been* (hadn't been able to be) at your baby's baptism.

219 present result following past condition

A present result clause containing *would* (*could* or *might*) + a base form can be combined with a past-unreal conditional (if) clause. In this kind of sentence, the event or nonevent in the *if* clause is the reason for the situation that is stated in the result clause:

past-unreal condition	*present result*
If we *hadn't missed* our train,	we *could be lying* on the beach right now instead of sitting in a station.
If they'*d paid* their income taxes,	they *wouldn't be* in a federal prison today.

220 *have to* and *be able to;* present versus past result

1. The idioms *have to* and *be able to* occasionally appear in present and past result clauses:

> If you had saved more money when you were younger, you *wouldn't have to be working* so hard now.
> If you'd been in the other class last semester, you *wouldn't have had to do* so much homework; the teacher was much easier than the one you had.
> If you had studied more during the past semester, you'*d be able to pass* the course and go on to the next level.
> If we hadn't run out of money on our trip, we *would have been able to go on* to San Francisco, but we had to go back to New York.

2. *Be able to* frequently appears in past-unreal conditions:

> If I'*d been able to get off* from work, I would have gone to my friend's wedding.

Have to may also occur in such clauses, but less frequently:

> If I *had had to go* out of town yesterday, I wouldn't have been able to see you.

221   special conditional form

In rather formal usage, we may drop the *if* in a conditional clause and place the auxiliary *had* before the subject as in a question form:

> *Had Adolph Hitler* not risen to power, World War II might not have taken place.
> *Had I* been in my bed during the earthquake, I would have gotten under it.

Note: A similar pattern with *were* in present conditionals may occur on rare occasions:

> *Were I* the president, I'd try to do more for the middle class.

222   questions

> **Reminder:** Like all other adverbial clauses, conditional clauses do not change in form in yes–no and information questions.

> *If you had gone to Europe last year*, would you have taken your family with you?
> What would you have done *if you'd been fired from your job?*

223   past real conditions

1. You will recall that real conditions are used to show a generalization about events that take place in present time with some kind of regularity. In this case *if* means *when:*

> *If* (when) we have guests for dinner, we always use our best silver and china.
> My roommate almost always carries a camera *if* (when) she goes on a trip.

2. Real conditions are also used for a generalization about an event that took place in past time. When this occurs, the past tense or its continuous form is used in both *if* and result clauses:

> During the meeting, *if* (when) my boss *wasn't* speaking, I *was;* no one else had anything to say.
> When I was a child, *if* (when) I *was* sick, I always *stayed* home from school.

3. *Used to* + a base form is also used in the result clause in such sentences:

When I was a boy, I *used to go* (*went*) hiking in the woods near our farm if I didn't have any chores to do, and my dog would always go with me.

My brother was very spoiled when he was small (he was the baby of the family); he always *used to cry* (*cried*) if he didn't get his own way.

4. Besides *used to* and the past tense, we may use *would* + a base form for past custom in the result clause:

When I was small, if my mother didn't tell me a bedtime story, my father *would tell* (*used to tell, told*) me one.

When our son was younger, he *would go* (*used to go, went*) to the movies on Saturday afternoon with his friends if he didn't have a baseball or football game to play.

5. When used for past custom, *would* and *used to* are not always interchangeable (particularly with the verb *be*). *Would* is never used for a general situation that once existed but no longer does. For example:

His mother *used to* (never *would*) be a famous opera singer.

We *used to* (never *would*) go dancing a lot, but now my wife and I would rather go jogging for our exercise.

That author *used to* (never *would*) write textbooks; now he writes romance novels.

224 *like;* expressing similarity

Linking verbs like *be, seem, look, act, feel, sound,* and *taste* followed by *like* are often used to express a similarity or a comparison:

This fabric *feels like* fine silk, but it's really synthetic.

Yes, she *looks like* a Persian cat, but I think she's a Maltese.

225 *like* versus *as*

1. Use *as* in a comparison beginning with *as, so,* or *such:*

I work *as* much *as* you do, but you make more money.

Life on the farm is not *so* difficult *as* it once was.

They like the exotic; they travel in *such* countries *as* India and China.

2. Use *as* to mean "in the role of" or "having the function of":

In her movies, Greta Garbo was always good *as* a tragic heroine, and she could be good in a comedy as well.

Mr. Smith is now acting *as* the president of the club while we prepare for a formal election next month.

-Ing forms may be used *as* gerunds or participles.

3. Use *as* for comparison when a subject and a verb phrase follow:

This chocolate tastes good *as* expensive chocolate should taste.
We're trying to do well *as* everyone else in this town is.

4. Use *like* in other kinds of comparisons:

I feel *like* a million dollars today.
She's got a hard job; she works *like* a slave.
Like the rest of us, the teacher has to work hard.

226   *as if* and *as though;* unreal opinions

1. We use *as if* and *as though* to introduce CLAUSES OF OPINION. If we feel our opinion is true or will probably come true, we use the customary tenses; for example, the present tense for present time, the future tense for future time:

It looks as if *we'll be leaving* tomorrow; we've finally gotten our exit visas.
She acts as though she *doesn't want* to go out with him.

The rule of sequence of tenses must be observed when the main verb is in its past form:

It looked as if *we would be leaving,* but then we couldn't get our visas.
She acted as though she *didn't want* to go out with him.

2. Usually, *as if* and *as though* introduce CLAUSES OF UNREAL OPINION. The verbs in these clauses take the same form as verbs following *if* in unreal conditions:

She's always acting as if she *were* a countess. (she's an actress and loves to pretend)
He sometimes looks as though he *had slept* in his clothes. (but I know his mother would never allow that)

However, there is no change in tenses when the main verb is in its past form:

She came into the room and acted as if she *were* a countess.
When I saw him on the street the other day, he looked as though he *had slept* in his clothes.

227 noun clauses derived from statements

1a. Reminder: A noun that is the DIRECT OBJECT of a verb usually tells *what*:

> He gave the customer *the bill*. (*What* did he give the customer?)
> She knit her grandson *a sweater*. (*What* did she knit her grandson?)

A noun that is the INDIRECT OBJECT of a verb usually tells *to* or *for* whom:

> He gave *the customer* the bill. (*To whom* did he give the bill?)
> She knit *her grandson* a sweater. (*For whom* did she knit a sweater?)

b. Reminder: The prepositions *to* and *for* are used only when a direct object follows the verb:

> He owes *his roommate* a favor (= He owes a favor *to his roommate*).
> Father made *us* a chocolate cake (= Father made a chocolate cake *for us*).

2. A NOUN CLAUSE always contains a verb and its subject. It functions as a noun and may occupy the same position in a sentence as a noun. For example, a noun clause can be used as the direct object of certain verbs:

> The judge has told *him* (indirect object) *that he must tell the truth* (direct object).

or as the subject of a sentence:

> *That we had lost the compass* was the main problem on our hike through the forest.

3. Noun clauses are derived from statements, questions, requests, and exclamations. A noun clause that is derived from a statement is introduced by the subordinate conjunction *that*:

> The *New York Times* reports *that* the situation is going to improve in the Middle East.

4. *That* is omitted in informal usage:

> The radio says (*that*) we're going to have a beautiful day.
> A prophet has predicted (*that*) the world will come to an end in the year 2000.

> **Reminder:** *That* clauses which follow adjectives of emotion and feeling have been classified as adverbial clauses in this textbook (see 200):
>
> All of us are pleased (Why?) *that we've made so much progress in the course.*

5. An indirect object may precede a noun clause that is a direct object:

> She's trying to teach *the students* (indirect object) *that getting to class on time is important. (direct object)*

or the noun clause may immediately follow the verb:

> She's trying to teach *that getting to class on time is important. (direct object)*

6. Noun clauses introduced by *that* may occur as direct objects of verbs called VERBS OF INDIRECT SPEECH. Some verbs of indirect speech are:

admit	complain	hint	remark	swear
announce	confess	mention	report	whisper
boast	declare	proclaim	say	
claim	explain	relate	state	

7. These verbs may be followed by *to* + indirect object + a *that* clause, or they may be immediately followed by a *that* clause:

> I'm always complaining (to my landlord) that the roof is leaking, but he doesn't ever do anything about it.
> My neighbor is always boasting (to me) that he has the most beautiful house in the neighborhood.

8. Some verbs of indirect speech, such as *(dis)agree, argue, forecast, maintain,* and *predict,* are not followed by a *to* phrase:

> We *agree* that the terms of this contract are not fair; we'll make some changes.
> The almanac *forecasts* a long winter ahead; be prepared.

9. The following verbs of indirect speech are always followed by an indirect object without *to:*

assure	inform	persuade	remind	tell
convince	notify	promise	teach	warn

For example:

> Don't forget to remind *me* that my favorite program comes on at nine.
> The radio has warned *travelers* that there are serious storm conditions in the mountains.

10. Noun clauses introduced by *that* are also used as direct objects of verbs that are called VERBS OF MENTAL ACTIVITY:

assume	decide	forget	know	realize
believe	discover	guess	learn	recall
calculate	doubt	hear	notice	regret
(don't) care	dream	hope	pretend	remember
conclude	feel	imagine	prove	think
consider	find out	indicate	question	understand

For example:

> Everyone in the world knows *that we must have peace in order to survive.*
>
> He's just found out *that he's won a million dollars in the lottery.*

11. A noun clause does not change in form when a statement is changed into a question:

> I believe *that people are basically good.*
>
> Do you believe *that people are basically good?*

228 noun clauses derived from yes-no questions; *whether*

1. In a noun clause derived from a yes–no question, the introductory word *whether* (or *if*) introduces the clause:

> We wonder *whether* (*if*) we will have good weather on our picnic.

Pronunciation note: *Whether* and *weather* have almost the same pronunciation.

2. When a noun clause is derived from a yes–no question, the subject precedes the verb, auxiliaries like *do* and *did* are dropped, and the question mark is dropped because the sentence is no longer a question:

> *original question*   *derivation*
>
> Does he live in Djakarta?   I don't know *whether he lives in Djakarta.*

However, the question mark is retained if the statement is a question:

> Does he live in Djakarta?   Do you know *whether he lives in Djakarta?*

3. *Whether* appears most frequently in formal usage:

> Everyone is wondering *whether* the government will raise taxes once again.

and *if* occurs in informal usage:

Everyone is wondering *if* the champion is going to be able to retain his title.

Reminder: *If* also introduces clauses of condition:

If I were a rich person, I really don't know what I'd do.

229   *whether* or *not*

1. The introductory word *whether* suggests a choice because it introduces a clause derived from a yes–no question. When a negative choice might be expected with *whether,* the words *or not* are added:

No one in the company knows *whether or not* we're going to go out of business.
We're still trying to decide *whether or not* we should adopt a baby.

2. For emphasis, *or not* occurs at the end of a noun clause if the clause is short:

We can't make up our minds *whether* we want to go shopping *or not.*
They don't know *whether* they're doing the right thing *or not.*

Note: In this pattern, *if* may replace *whether,* but only in very informal usage:

We don't know *if* we'll run out of money *or not,* so we're being careful.

230   noun clauses derived from information questions

1. When a noun clause is derived from an information question, an information word (or words) introduces the clause:

A gambler never knows *how much money he's going to win or lose.*
Some of the students don't know *what the formula for this chemical is.*

2. In a noun clause derived from an information question, the subject of the clause follows the information word. The subject never follows an auxiliary in a noun clause, and the auxiliary *do* is dropped. Also, if the clause is being used in a statement, the question mark is dropped.

original question	*derivation*
What kind of work does he do?	I wonder *what kind of work he does.*
What time is it?	Would you happen to know *what time it is?*

Reminder: When a noun clause occurs in a yes–no question, the form of the clause does not change. Compare:

statement	*question*
I don't know *where the elevators are.*	Do you know *where the elevators are?*
I wonder *how much my boss makes.*	Do you *know how much my boss makes?*

231   the rule of sequence of tenses

1. The RULE OF SEQUENCE OF TENSES states that a verb in a subordinate clause must agree with the verb in the main clause of a complex sentence. It is necessary to follow this rule in a sentence containing a noun clause when the verb in the main clause is in its past form:

I *didn't know* what time it *was,* so I turned on the radio.
She *didn't know* how many mistakes she'*d made,* so she couldn't figure out the score.

2. Study the following to see what changes are made when noun clauses are derived from statements and questions and when the verb in the main clause of the sentence is in its past form:

a. The present tense is changed to the past tense:

I *live* in the country. She *said* that she *lived* in the country.

b. The present continuous tense is changed to the past continuous tense:

Are you *living* in the city? She *asked* me if I *was* living in the city.

c. The past tense is changed to the past perfect tense:

Did I *lock* the door? I *wondered* whether I'*d locked* the door or not.

d. The past continuous tense is changed to the past perfect continuous tense:

He *was working* outside. *Did* he *say* that he'*d been working* outside?

e. The present perfect (continuous) tense is changed to the past perfect (continuous) tense:

We'*ve fixed* it. They said they'*d fixed* it.
We'*ve been fixing* it. They said they'*d been fixing* it.

3. We do not follow the rule of sequence of tenses when the main verb is in a present form:

She *says* that she *lived* in the country when she was a child.
He *has said* that he's *living* in the city.

232 the rule of sequence of tenses; modals

1. When following the rule of sequence of tenses, past forms of modal auxiliaries are used in dependent clauses of indirect speech to agree with the past form of the main verb:

a. *Can* is changed to *could:*

I *can* do it. I said that I *could do* it.

b. *May* is changed to *might:*

May we sit down? They asked if they *might* sit down.

c. *Must* is changed to *had to:*

What time must I go? He wanted to know what time he *had to* go.

d. *Will* is changed to *would:*

We will succeed. We all hoped that we *would* succeed.

e. *Shall* is changed to *would:*

I *shall* return. MacArthur said that he *would* return.

2. *Ought to*, *should*, and *might* do not change form in dependent clauses of indirect speech. They are considered to express the same time as the main verb:

You *should* sit down. I said that you *should* sit down. (*not* should have sat down)
I *might* be late. I told them I *might* be late. (*not* might have been)

These three modals also express time future to the main verb:

I *should* go tomorrow. I said that I *should* go the following day. (*not* should have gone)
I *might* be here next week. I told them I *might* be here the following week. (*not* might have been)

233-237 indirect speech

1. DIRECT SPEECH is a speaker's exact words. In direct speech, quotation marks (") are used in the written language:

Winston Churchill said, "The sun will never set on the British Empire."

INDIRECT SPEECH (reported speech) is the restatement of the speaker's original words:

> Winston Churchill said that the sun would never set on the British Empire.

2. In indirect speech, the quoted material is most often a noun clause. Quotation marks are not used, and the pronouns and possessive adjectives are usually transformed from one person to another. Quite frequently, so that the statement may remain logical, verbs in the noun clause are changed into past forms in accordance with the rule of sequence of tenses. Compare:

a. He said, "*I'm* thinking about buying *myself* a car."
He said that *he* was thinking about buying *himself* a car.

b. She asked, "Did *you* receive a message for *me?*"
She asked me if *I* had received a message for *her*.

c. They wrote, "*We're* going to invite *you* to *our* house soon."
They wrote that *they* were going to invite *me* to *their* house soon.

3. Often, when we are following the rule of sequence of tenses, there may be more than one tense change in a single sentence:

> He said, "I *may* not be able to go because I *don't* have any money."
> He said he *might* not be able to go because he *didn't* have any money.

4. *Say* and *tell* make a frequent appearance in indirect speech. When *say* is followed by an indirect object, the preposition *to* is always used. Compare:

correct	*incorrect*
She said *to me* that she was ready.	She said [me] that she was ready.
I'm saying *to you* that I'm your friend.	I'm saying [you] that I'm your friend.

Tell is followed by an indirect object without *to:*

correct	*incorrect*
Tell *me* that you care for me.	Tell [to me] that you care for me.
They're telling *us* to be quiet.	They're telling [to us] to be quiet.

5. Although the verb *tell* usually requires an indirect object without *to*, *tell* also occurs in certain idioms, with or without an indirect object:

a. tell a story: Please tell (us) the story of your life, Professor.
b. tell a riddle: How many riddles has the class joker told (us) today?

    c. tell a secret: Promise not to tell (anyone) this secret; it's between you and me.

    d. tell the truth: Will you swear on the Bible to tell (us) the truth?

    e. tell a lie: Someone has been telling (us) lies about the government scandal.

    f. tell a fortune: The gypsy will tell (you) your fortune for a dollar.

    g. tell the time: By using only the sun, can you tell (me) the time?

6. A *to* phrase may follow the verb *say:*

    I'm always saying *to myself* that I must strive to be good.

However, the phrase is usually omitted because an indirect object is understood or not necessary:

    She's always saying she doesn't love him, but he knows that she does.
    I said I had some extra money in my pocket, and I'd like to take you out to dinner.

7. Students sometimes confuse the verbs *speak* and *talk* with *say* and *tell.*

    a. *Speak* can mean to *greet:*

    When I see her on the street, she always speaks to me (says hello).

Speak is also used in reference to certain formal situations. Note the following sentences:

    The President had spoken (discussed) with his advisors before the final decision was made.
    The preacher is speaking (giving a sermon) about the concept of original sin.
    The professor is going to speak (give a lecture) about the practical applications of linguistics.

Speak is always used with the names of languages:

    How many languages can you speak? English is spoken here.

    b. *Talk* is used when we are referring to a conversation between two or more people:

    What are you two talking about (you look very secretive)?
    When the teacher walked into the room, the students were talking about her.

Talk is almost never followed by a direct object except in a very few idioms:

    Let's talk business.
    Let's talk shop (business).
    They're talking treason.

8. The verb *ask* is always followed by an indirect object without *to:*

Ask *me* no questions and I'll tell you no lies. (old saying)

The indirect object after *ask* may be omitted when it is understood:

Our children are always asking (us) why they need a baby-sitter.

238-239 indirect speech; the distant past

1. In indirect speech, particularly when we are speaking of events in the DISTANT PAST, the various words and expressions of time, place, and modification used in direct speech must be changed so that they logically agree with the rule of sequence of tenses. Compare:

direct speech	*indirect speech*
He said, "I'll be *here next week*."	He said that he'd be *there the following week.*
She said, "I ate several hours *ago*."	She said she'd eaten several hours *earlier.*

2. However, when we make a statement about an event that has taken place in the NEAR PAST, a change need not be made because confusion is less likely to occur. Compare:

near past	*distant past*
When I spoke to him a few minutes *ago* (he's just left the office), he said he'd be *here next week.*	When I'd spoken to him a few minutes *earlier* (this was almost a month ago), he said he'd be there the *following week.*

3. When we make a statement about an event in the distant past, most of the usual changes to be made are:

    a. *ago* to *before/earlier*

    b. *now* to *then*

    c. *here* to *there*

    d. *this/these* to *that/those*

    e. *today/tonight* to *that day/that night*

    f. *yesterday* to *the day before/the previous day*

    g. *tomorrow* to *the following day* (formal)/*the next day* (informal)

    h. *last week/last month/last year* to *the week/month/year before*

    i. *tomorrow morning/afternoon/evening/night* to *the following (next) morning/afternoon/evening/night*

    j. *next week/month/year* to *the following week/month/year*

4. In less formal usage, the rule of sequence of tenses is often not observed in indirect speech, particularly when we make a statement about the *near past:*

> I *was* just telling him (a few minutes ago) that he *is* doing a great job.
> I just *told* my boss (ten minutes or so ago) that I *am* taking this afternoon off.

Also, the rule of sequence of tenses is not observed if we are expressing a universal truth:

> The little girl *said* two and two *are* four.
> The teacher *said* that the shortest distance between two points *is* a straight line.

or if we are discussing a customary event:

> He *told* us that he always *goes* to bed at nine in the evening.
> She *said* that she usually *gets* out of the office around five.

240 commands in indirect speech

1. Sentences in the imperative mood (commands) in direct speech are changed in indirect speech to infinitive phrases which are the direct object of the main verb of a sentence. Compare:

direct	*indirect*
She said, "Be kind to me."	She told him *to be kind to her.*
I said, "Remember me."	I asked her *to remember me.*

Note: As in indirect statements and questions, quotation marks are not used in indirect commands.

2. In negative commands, the auxiliary *do* is dropped in indirect speech, and the adverb *not* precedes the infinitive. Compare:

direct	*indirect*
They said, "Don't use our books."	They told us *not to use* their books.
We said, "Don't pick on us."	We told them *not to pick on us.*

3. When *please* occurs in a direct command, it is omitted in indirect speech:

direct	*indirect*
He said, "Please be my wife."	He asked her *to be* his wife.
I said, "Please don't talk about me."	I asked you *not to talk* about me.

4. Proper names that appear in direct commands often become indirect objects of the main verb of an indirect statement. Compare:

direct	*indirect*
He said, "Anna, call your brother."	He *told Anna* to call her brother.
She said, "Don't speak to me, Tim."	She *told Tim* not to speak to her.

241   noun clauses derived from exclamations

1. Noun clauses derived from exclamations are introduced by *what* (*a*) or *how*. The word order remains the same in such derivations:

exclamation	*derivation*
How rich he is!	He's always boasting about *how rich he is.*
What greedy people they are!	They don't realize *what greedy people they are.*
What a beautiful day it is!	Everyone is talking about *what a beautiful day it is.*

2. These clauses may occur as objects of verbs or of prepositions. The verbs that they most frequently follow are a few verbs of mental activity such as *notice, observe, realize, remember, see, forget,* and *understand:*

> Did you see *how big the elephant in the parade was?*
> I don't think you understand *what a serious mistake you've made.*

3. When clauses derived from exclamations occur as objects of prepositions, they follow certain verbs of indirect speech combined with the preposition *about—boast about, complain about, talk about,* and *remark about:*

> He's always *boasting about* what beautiful and intelligent children he has.
> Some of the students are complaining about *how difficult the homework is.*

Such clauses may also follow the noun forms of these verbs:

> My neighbor is also very boastful about *how beautiful and clever his wife is.*
> Excuse me, I have a complaint about *how poor the service in this restaurant is.*

4. Noun clauses derived from exclamations also follow such *-ed* participial adjectives of emotion as *astonished, disappointed, disgusted, pleased,* and *surprised.* These verbs are usually combined with the preposition *at;* a noun clause is the object of the preposition:

> Everyone is pleased at *how much progress they've made in the course.*
> I was surprised at *what an important job my roommate had found.*

242 infinitives following information words

1. Certain verbs are followed by two-part direct objects consisting of an information word (or words) and an infinitive (phrase):

> Do you know *how to type?*
> They don't know *whom to invite* to their party.

2. This pattern is also used with some verbs that require an indirect object:

> Can you tell *me* how to get to the top of the company?
> Mother, could you show *me* how to make a paper plane?

243 *that* noun clauses after verbs of urgency

1. Like noun clauses derived from statements, noun clauses derived from requests are introduced by *that. That* is optional.

> The police demanded (*that*) *we show our identification in order to pass through the barricades.*
> The opposition party insists (*that*) *the President be impeached.*

2. Noun clauses derived from requests most often occur after verbs called VERBS OF URGENCY (request verbs):

advise	demand	insist	recommend	require	suggest
ask	desire	propose	request	stipulate	urge

3. The verb in a *that* clause following a verb of urgency is a base form (traditionally called the present subjunctive):

> Everyone in the class has suggested to the teacher that he *call off* the final examination.

Not precedes the base form in negative verb phrases:

> The directions on the label advise that this fabric *not be* washed in hot water.

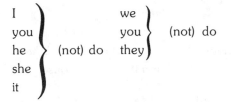

4. The verb *be* also remains a base form in all persons:

> The President has suggested that everyone's taxes *be* cut by 10 percent.

5. The verb in a *that* clause derived from a request remains a base form regardless of the tense of the verb in the main clause:

> My lawyer recommends (recommended) that I *take up* this matter with my senator in Washington, D.C.
> The people demand (demanded) that the political prisoners *be* released.

6. Following the verbs *recommend, advise,* or *suggest, should* sometimes occurs in less formal usage:

> His attorney recommended (or advised, suggested) that he *should* leave the country at once.

244 *that* noun clauses after adjectives of urgency

That clauses occasionally follow certain adjectives which are called ADJECTIVES OF URGENCY. A verb in this kind of clause takes the same form as a verb in a *that* clause following a verb of urgency:

> It is absolutely necessary that everyone in the country *pay* his or her fair share of the taxes.
> It is essential that dedicated people *be* elected to public office.

Some adjectives of urgency are:

advisable	better	essential	imperative	mandatory	urgent
best	desirable	good	important	necessary	vital

245 *wish* in the present

1. Like the past tense after *if* in an unreal condition, the past tense in a *that* clause after *wish* expresses a wish that is contrary to fact or reality. Compare:

reality	*wish*
We don't have a car.	We wish that we *had* a car.
We have termites in our house.	We wish that we *didn't have* termites in our house.

2. As in *if* clauses in unreal conditions, if *be* is the verb in a *that* clause after *wish* the special (subjunctive) form *were* is used in all persons:

I wish that I *were* a rich person so that I could help the poor children of my town.

I wish that there *were* more time in a day; I can never get all my work done.

3. In less formal usage, *that* is omitted:

I wish (that) I knew how to speak and write English as well as my teacher.

4. Continuous forms may occur in *that* clauses after *wish:*

The children wish it *weren't raining* now so that they could go out and play.

I wish that I *were going* away this summer, but I can't afford to.

5. *Didn't have to* + a base form occurs in a *that* clause after wish to express *it is not necessary:*

reality	*wish*
He has to work hard.	He wishes that he *didn't have to work* hard.
She has to take the dog for a walk.	She wishes she *didn't have to take* the dog for a walk.

Note: In the simple present tense, *wish* followed by an infinitive means *to want:*

The Prime Minister wishes (wants) to consult the Minister of Defense.

However, *wish,* meaning *to want* is usually heard in rather formal usage.

246   *wish* in the past

1. Like the past perfect tense in an *if* clause in a past-unreal condition, the past perfect tense in a *that* clause after *wish* expresses a wish that is contrary to fact or reality in past time. Compare:

Past Reality: I parked my car in front of a fire hydrant. (I got a ticket)
Wish: I wish that I *hadn't parked* my car in front of a fire hydrant. (I wouldn't have gotten a ticket if I hadn't)
Past Reality: She didn't have time to do her homework last night. (She's doing poorly in class today)
Wish: She wishes that she *had had* time to do her homework last night. (If she had, she wouldn't be making so many mistakes now)

2. Statements containing *wish* + a *that* clause referring to past time are made in response to an event or situation that takes place in either present or past time:

situation	wish
I'm losing my money.	I wish I *hadn't started* gambling.
My car broke down yesterday.	I wish that I *hadn't ever bought* it.

247 *wish* with *could;* past and present

1. In present time, *could* is used in a *that* clause after *wish* to express ability or possibility:

I wish I *could afford* to take a vacation this year; if I could, I would go to Europe.
I wish I *could* work miracles; I'd make millions if I could, but I can't.

2. *Could have* (+ *been*) + a past participle is used in *that* clauses after wish to express ability or possibility in past time:

I wish I *could have gone* out dancing last Saturday night, but my parents dropped in on me by surprise; I had to stay home and entertain them.
We wish the job *could have been done* more quickly, but we'd had some difficulties in getting the right kind of supplies.

Note: *Couldn't have* almost never occurs in *that* clauses after *wish*.

248 *wish* with *would;* future

1. *Wish* followed by a *that* clause containing the simple past tense or the past perfect tense expresses a condition that is unreal; however, *wish* followed by a verb phrase with *would* + a base form represents a wish that is possible to realize. Compare:

contrary to reality	*possible to realize*
(The baby is crying.)	
I wish she weren't crying.	I wish she *would stop* crying.
(John isn't in love with Mary.)	
She wishes he were in love with her.	She wishes he *would fall* in love with her.

2. Wishes with *would* are sometimes used to make a polite request:

> I wish you *would please sit down* and take it easy for a while.
> Jennifer, I wish you *would stop* teasing the kittens so much.

249   *hope*

1. Usually, we *hope* for events that may take place in the future, using a *that* clause following the verb *hope:*

> All of us hope (*that*) *we'll get a good grade in the course.*
> The Prime Minister hopes (*that*) *she will be reelected.*

2. Often, we express an *unrealized hope* in past time with the verb *hope* followed by *would* + a base form in a *that* clause:

> Adolph Hitler hoped that he *would conquer* the world.
> Ponce de León hoped that he *would find* the fountain of youth.
> Karl Marx hoped that the workers of the world *would unite.*
> Ferdinand Magellan hoped that he *would go* around the world.

3. When we express a hope that is related to ourselves, we may use either an infinitive phrase or a *that* clause—*that* is optional.

> I hope *to see you soon.*   I hope (*that*) *I'll see you soon.*
> I hope *to make a million.*   I hope (*that*) *I'll make a million.*

4. When we express a hope that in *not* related to ourselves, only a *that* clause may be used:

> I hope *that* all my classmates will enjoy a long, happy, and prosperous life.
> Everyone in the world hopes *that* there will eventually be peace on earth.

> **Note:** In sentences with *hope* for the future (paragraphs 1, 3, and 4), with certain verbs the present and future tenses may be used interchangeably:
>
> I hope that I *meet* some nice people on my vacation.
> I hope that I'll *meet* some nice people on my vacation.

We hope that our children *have* lots of luck.
We hope that our children *will have* lots of luck.

Sometimes, the present tense or its continuous form can refer to present or future time:

I hope you're happy. (now)   I hope you're happy. (in
                                                                     the future)
I hope you're feeling well. (now)   I hope you're feeling well.
                                                                     (tomorrow)

5. When we express a hope about the PRESENT UNKNOWN, we use one of the present tenses:

I hope my old school friends *are* happy. (I haven't seen or heard from them for years)
We hope no one *has lost* his way. (Why haven't our guests arrived?)
I hope they're *living* a happy life. (the last time I saw them was ten years ago)

6. When we express a hope about the PAST UNKNOWN, we use the simple past tense or its continuous form:

He hopes that no one *saw* him when he stole the money.
She hopes that her boss *didn't see* her when she came into the office late today.
I hope that I *wasn't making* a mistake when I put an X in the blank.

250   abridgement of noun clause after *wish*

Commonly, an abridgement of a *that* clause after *wish* occurs in a statement which is in response to another statement made by either ourselves or another person:

Rarely is life easy. I wish *that it were.*
Dick has to do a lot of chores every morning. He wishes *he didn't.*
Our teacher can't work miracles. All of us in the class wish *he could.*
We couldn't go out last night. We wish *we could have.*
I didn't eat much for breakfast. I wish *I had.*
We weren't at the picnic. We wish *we had been.*

Note: When the simple past form of the verb *be* occurs in the initial statement, *been* always follows the auxiliary *had* in an abridgement after *wish:*

There were no friends of mine at the meeting. I wish there *had been.*
Dinner was served very late. I wish it *hadn't been.*

251   *who* and *that* as subjects of essential adjective clauses

1. An ADJECTIVE CLAUSE is a subordinate clause that modifies a noun or pronoun, which precedes it in the main clause of a sentence:

> He *who laughs last* laughs best. (old saying)
> People *who live in glass houses* shouldn't throw stones. (old saying)

2. The noun or pronoun that is modified by an adjective clause is called the ANTECEDENT of that clause:

> "*The man* who murdered the heiress is standing there," Sherlock Holmes said as he pointed at the butler.
> Look at these beautiful apples! Why don't you take *those* that are best to your teacher?

> **Note:** Adjective clauses are sometimes called RELATIVE CLAUSES. The British often refer to them as DEFINING CLAUSES.

3. An adjective clause frequently "splits" the main clause of a sentence:

> The watch *that I'm wearing* I inherited from my grandfather.
> Ladies and Gentlemen, the person *who has solved the riddle* will win a thousand dollars.

4. Adjective clauses are most often introduced by the relative pronoun *who* (*whom* or *whose*) or *that*. *Who* is usually used in reference to a person, and *that* refers to an animal or thing:

> Did you know the man *who* is standing in front of you is the President?
> I'm looking for a store *that* buys and sells used books.

However, in less formal usage *that* may be used to refer to a person:

> The woman *that* he marries must be able to put up with his short temper.

When we are referring to animal pets, or when we are personifying an animal, we may use *who*:

> We have a pet parrot *who* is always talking to himself.
> The dog *who* is living upstairs is a darling poodle, but she's always barking.

5. We often use *who* or *that* as the subject of an adjective clause. It replaces the subject that originally appears in the sentence from which the clause is derived:

I know a man. *He* can tell fortunes = I know a man *who* can tell fortunes.

She has a watch. *It* has no hands = She has a watch *that* has no hands.

6. There are two kinds of adjective clauses: ESSENTIAL and NONESSENTIAL CLAUSES. An essential adjective clause cannot be omitted from a sentence, because the true meaning of the sentence would be lost; for example, if the adjective clause is omitted from the sentence *People who commit crime should be sent to jail*, the remaining main clause *People . . . should be sent to jail* is false. Compare:

essential adjective clause	*false statement*
Children *who have a highly contagious disease* should not be with other children.	Children . . . should not be with other children.
Babies *who are allergic to milk* shouldn't be fed milk.	Babies . . . shouldn't be fed milk.

Punctuation note: Essential adjective clauses are *never* set off with commas.

252 *whose* introducing essential adjective clauses

When *whose* is used to introduce an adjective clause, it is always followed by a noun:

I know a man *whose daughter* won a gold medal at the Olympics.
We have a neighbor *whose dog* is always chasing our cat.

253 nonessential adjective clauses; *which*

1. In a sentence containing a nonessential adjective clause, the adjective clause may be omitted from the sentence because the truth of the statement would not be lost; for example, if the adjective clause is omitted from the sentence *Exercise, which we all need, is good for you*, the remaining main clause *Exercise . . . is good for you* remains a true statement. Compare:

nonessential clause	*true statement*
Life, *which is going by too fast*, is wonderful.	Life . . . is wonderful.
Time, *which I never seem to have enough of*, goes by fast.	Time . . . goes by fast.

Punctuation note: Nonessential adjective clauses are *always* set off with commas in writing and pauses in speech:

> Abraham Lincoln, (pause) *who was born in a log cabin,* (pause) eventually became the President of the United States.

2. The relative pronoun *that* is the usual marker for essential clauses following an antecedent that refers to a thing; however, the relative pronoun *which* sometimes occurs:

> They have a house *that* (*which*) has a fabulous view of the Pacific Ocean.
> I'm looking for a machine *that* (*which*) makes ice.

3. We never use *that* to introduce nonessential clauses; they are introduced by *which:*

> Today, *which* happens to be my birthday, is going to be my wedding day.
> Life on a farm, *which* is wonderful for children, can be hard for adults.

4. Nonessential adjective clauses may also be said to provide extra information that can be left in or out of a sentence:

> My house, *which is just around the corner,* is a cozy little place.
> CO, *which is the formula for carbon monoxide,* is an easy formula to remember.

5. Adjective clauses following proper nouns are always nonessential:

> Adam and Eve, *who were the first man and woman,* didn't listen to God's command.
> Christopher Columbus, *who didn't know where he was when he landed in the New World,* mistakenly called the indigenous people Indians.

6. An essential adjective clause is traditionally called a RESTRICTIVE CLAUSE because it restricts, singles out, or defines the antecedent in the main clause of a sentence; it refers to *some* of a class. A nonessential clause is traditionally called NONRESTRICTIVE because it does not restrict, single out, or define the antecedent; it refers to *all* of a class. Compare:

essential *(restrictive), some*	*nonessential* *(nonrestrictive), all*
The magazines that are not current must be thrown away.	The magazines, which are not current, must be thrown away.
The students who have done well should get a good grade.	The students, who have done well, should get a good grade.

7. Essential adjective clauses are often used to define a part of a class:

> A cannibal (a part) is a person (a class) *who eats the flesh of human beings.*
>
> A dog (a part) is an animal (a class) *that enjoys being with humans.*

8. We often express contrast or concession with nonessential clauses:

> T. J. Clark, who has already made a million dollars this year, wants to make a million more. (Even though he's made a million, he wants to make a million more.)
>
> Our team, which is the worst in the league, won the championship. (Even though our team is the worst in the league, it won the championship.)

254 relative pronouns as objects of verbs and prepositions

1. As we have already discussed, relative pronouns may be used as subjects of adjective clauses:

> The people *who* developed the wheel started the world rolling.
>
> How exciting! The number in the lottery *that* won the prize is mine; I'm suddenly a millionaire.

2. Relative pronouns may also be used as the object of a verb:

> The man *whom* she met at the reception was some famous person in the world of music.

or as the object of a preposition:

> The man *to whom* she was introduced at the reception eventually became her husband.

3. When a relative pronoun is the object of a verb or preposition, a formal or informal style may be used. Without a doubt, the informal style is most frequently observed. Only in formal writing does the formal style usually occur. Compare:

formal	*informal*
object of a verb	
The woman *whom he married* was the perfect companion for him.	The woman *who he married* was the perfect companion for him.
The lawyer *whom we consulted* didn't know what he was talking about.	The lawyer *who we consulted* didn't know what he was talking about.

object of a preposition

The woman *at whom he was swearing* was his secretary.	The woman *who he was swearing at* was his secretary.
The man *for whom I voted* didn't win the election.	The man *who I voted for* didn't win the election.

Note: Study the use of postponed prepositions in informal usage (see 44).

255   unmarked essential adjective clauses

In informal usage, when a relative pronoun in an adjective clause is the object of a verb or a preposition, the pronoun may be omitted. The clause then becomes what is called an UNMARKED ADJECTIVE CLAUSE:

The religion (that) *she practices forbids the use of alcohol.*
The person (who) *I work for doesn't ever give me a hard time.*

Note: Since a clause always has a subject, a relative pronoun cannot be omitted from a clause when the pronoun is the subject of the clause:

He *who* gets the highest score wins the game.
They have a pet monkey *that* is always playing with their dog.

256   *where* introducing essential adjective clauses

1. The relative adverb *where* is frequently used to introduce essential adjective clauses:

I don't enjoy being in a place *where my presence is not wanted.*
They're looking for a city *where the standard of living is high and the cost of living is low.*

2. *After, before,* and *why* are three other words that sometimes introduce adjective clauses:

We left Amsterdam the day *after our friends arrived.*
He quit his job at the company on the day *before he was to receive a big promotion and raise.*
Please give me a good reason *why you didn't show up for work yesterday.*

257 the present perfect and past perfect tenses in essential adjective clauses

1. When the object of a verb in a main clause is a noun modified by a superlative adjective (This is *the best hamburger*), it is frequently followed by an adjective clause containing *ever* in a verb phrase in the present perfect tense:

> "This is the best hamburger *that I've ever eaten,*" the little boy said.

This kind of clause is usually introduced by *that,* but its use is optional:

> Without a doubt, this is the most comfortable bed (*that*) *I've ever slept on.*
>
> My boss is one of the nicest people (*that*) *I've ever met,* fortunately.

2. The past perfect tense also sometimes makes an appearance in the same pattern (note how the rule of sequence of tenses must be followed here):

> What a fantastic movie! It was the best science-fiction film (*that*) *I'd ever seen.*
>
> What a fabulous country we were in last summer! It was one of the most enjoyable vacations (*that*) *we'd ever had.*

258 causatives with *have* + actor + base form + object

1. CAUSATIVE FORMS are used when one person causes another to perform a service—in other words, gives instructions to someone else. The following pattern is causative: Causer (person who causes the action) + *have* + actor (doer or performing agent) + base form + object. For example:

> I (causer) have my son (actor) pick up (base form) the newspaper (object) for me every afternoon on his way home from school.

2. Since causative forms are used when it is necessary to take a particular course of action, *have to,* the idiomatic substitute for *must,* often occurs in causative verb phrases in all the six tenses:

> Present Tense: I *have to* have the jeweler put a new band on my wrist watch.
>
> Past Tense: He *had to* have a plumber put new plumbing in the kitchen.
>
> Future Tense: I'll *have to* have someone fix the roof of my house; it's been leaking lately.

Present Perfect Tense: We *have had to* have a repairman come to our house at least five times to fix the TV that we bought only a year ago.

Past Perfect Tense: They were depressed and unhappy because they *had had to* have the veterinarian destroy their pet dog.

Future Perfect Tense: I'll *have had to* have a lot of people fix up things around here by the time this project is completed.

3. Modals and idiomatic substitutes also often occur in causative patterns:

You *must* have someone check this report over.

That was a difficult job; you *must* have had to have someone help you.

I've *got to* have the electrician check something in the garage.

You'd *better* have a mechanic look at this car before you buy it.

259 causatives with *have* + object + past participle

1. When the actor is not mentioned in a causative, a past participle replaces the base form, and the object precedes the verb rather than following it:

The president of the company (causer) had (actor not mentioned) three of the company's vice presidents (object) fired (past participle).

2. As with other causative forms, the idiom *have to* may occur in all the tenses:

Do you *have to* have your house painted, or are you going to do it yourself?

How many times *had* you *had to* have your car fixed since you bought it?

Did you *have to* have a new roof put on your house after the hurricane?

260 causatives with *get* + object + past participle

1. In the pattern illustrated in 259, *get* may replace *have:*

The president of the company *got* three of the company's vice presidents fired.

Note: *Get* cannot replace *have* in the pattern illustrated in 258.

261 persuasion with *get* + object + infinitive

1. *Get* + object + infinitive is another causative form, which is used to express persuasion. It usually occurs in questions:

> How do you *get your children to be* so neat and tidy?
> How does your neighbor *get her flowers to grow* so quickly?

2. *Not* precedes the infinitive in negative phrases:

> How did you get your roommate *not to tell* the secret?
> How did you get your cat and dog *not to fight?*

Index